Apple Augmented Reality by Tutorials

By Chris Language

Apple Augmented Reality by Tutorials

Chris Language

Copyright ©2020 Razeware LLC.

Notice of Rights

All rights reserved. No part of this book or corresponding materials (such as text, images, or source code) may be reproduced or distributed by any means without prior written permission of the copyright owner.

Notice of Liability

This book and all corresponding materials (such as source code) are provided on an "as is" basis, without warranty of any kind, express of implied, including but not limited to the warranties of merchantability, fitness for a particular purpose, and noninfringement. In no event shall the authors or copyright holders be liable for any claim, damages or other liability, whether in action of contract, tort or otherwise, arising from, out of or in connection with the software or the use of other dealing in the software.

Trademarks

All trademarks and registered trademarks appearing in this book are the property of their own respective owners.

ISBN: 978-1-950325-21-4

About the Authors

Chris Language is the author of this book. Chris is a seasoned coder with 20+ years of experience, and the author of 3D Apple Games by Tutorials. He has fond memories of his childhood and his Commodore 64; more recently he started adding more good memories of life with all his Apple devices. By day, he fights for survival in the corporate jungle of Johannesburg, South Africa. By night he fights demons, dragons and zombies! For relaxation, he codes. You can find him on Twitter @ChrisLanguage Forever Coder, Artist, Musician, Gamer and Dreamer.

About the Editors

Tammy Coron is the final pass editor of this book. Tammy is an independent creative professional. As an author, editor, illustrator, podcaster, and indie game developer, Tammy spends a lot of her time creating content and teaching others. For more information about Tammy, visit her website at tammycoron.com.

Sandra Grauschopf is the editor of this book. Sandra is the Editing Team Lead at raywenderlich.com. She's an experienced writer, editor, and content manager who loves to explore the world with a book in her hand.

About the Artist

Vicki Wenderlich is the designer and artist of the cover of this book. She is Ray's wife and business partner. She is a digital artist who creates illustrations, game art and a lot of other art or design work for the tutorials and books on raywenderlich.com. When she's not making art, she loves hiking, a good glass of wine and attempting to create the perfect cheese plate.

Table of Contents

Book License 13

Before You Begin 15

What You Need 17

Book Source Code & Forums 19

Introduction 21
    How to read this book 21

Section I: Reality Composer 23

Chapter 1: AR Quick Start 25
    Creating an AR project with Xcode 26
    Exploring the project 27
    Asking for camera permission 29
    Adding custom assets 30
    Presenting the custom scene 33
    Setting up the UI 34
    Adding tank animations 40
    Parenting entities 41
    Adding turret animations 41
    Final touches 42
    Key points 44

Chapter 2: AR Quick Look 45
    What is AR Quick Look? 46
    AR Quick Look features 46
    AR Quick Look limitations 48
    Experiencing AR Quick Look 48
    AR Quick Look for web 51
    AR Quick Look for apps 53

Key points 58
Where to go from here? 58

Chapter 3: Reality Composer & Reality Files 59
What is Reality Composer? 60
Reality Composer features 62
Reality Composer's limitations 63
Creating Reality Composer projects 64
Exploring the UI 66
Adding scenes 67
Navigating scenes 69
Adding objects 70
Adjusting object transforms 72
Adjusting object properties 73
Enabling physics 75
Playing scenes 77
What are Reality files? 77
Key points 80

Chapter 4: USDZ Files & USD Python Tools 81
What is USD? 81
What is USDZ? 83
USDZ tools 83
Reviewing the project 86
Exporting 3D models 87
Converting 3D models to USDZ 93
Converting USDZ to USDA 94
Inspecting and validating USDZ 95
Importing USDZ assets 97
Key points 100
Where to go from here? 100

Chapter 5: Reality Converter & PBR Materials 101

- What is Reality Converter? 102
- Adding a 3D model 102
- PBR materials 104
- Environment 109
- Properties 112
- Sharing 112
- Exporting USDZ 113
- Key points 114

Section II: Reality Composer & Image Tracking 115

Chapter 6: Image Anchors 117
- What are image anchors? 118
- Creating an image anchor project 119
- Adding an image 123
- Adding 3D text 127
- Completing the scene 129
- Editing on iOS 130
- Key points 134

Chapter 7: Behaviors, Triggers & Actions 135
- What are behaviors? 136
- What are triggers? 137
- What are actions? 138
- Adding a behavior preset 140
- Adding action sequences 142
- Adding custom behaviors 151
- Duplicating behaviors 154
- Challenge yourself 156
- Key points 157

Section III: Reality Composer & Object Tracking . 159

Chapter 8: Object Anchors 161

Crafting a toy truck 161
What are object anchors? 163
Installing the 3D object scanner 163
Preparing for 3D object scanning 165
Scanning 3D objects 166
Testing and improving 3D scans 171
Exporting AR objects 174
Creating object anchors 175
Key points 178

Section IV: RealityKit & Face Tracking 179

Chapter 9: RealityKit 181
What is RealityKit? 182
Creating a RealityKit project 183
RealityKit API components 189
Building the UI with SwiftUI 190
Taking selfies 194
Key points 197
Where to go from here? 197

Chapter 10: Face Anchors 199
What are face anchors? 200
Creating face anchors 201
Creating multiple scenes 203
Code generation 207
Fixing the project 208
Switching to the front-facing camera 208
Switching between multiple scenes 210
Testing the app 211
Manually removing anchors 212
Key points 213

Chapter 11: Facial Blend Shapes 215

What are facial blend shapes? 216
Building the robot 217
Adding the new robot scene 220
Using the ARSessionDelegate protocol 222
Adding ARDelegateHandler 223
Handling ARSession updates 224
Tracking blinking eyes 225
Tracking eyebrows 225
Tracking the jaw 226
Positioning with quaternions 226
Updating the eyelids 227
Updating the jaw 229
Adding lasers 230
Sending & receiving notifications 232
Key points 237

Section V: ARKit & SpriteKit 239

Chapter 12: ARKit 241
What is ARKit? 242
ARKit-powered app examples 246
ARKit's features 248
ARKit's limitations 252
ARKit resources 254
Key points 256

Chapter 13: ARKit & SpriteKit 257
What is SpriteKit? 258
Creating a SpriteKit AR project 258
Exploring the project 261
ARSKView & ARSession 265
Creating a heads-up display (HUD) 265
Adding game state 268

Creating a spawn point 271
ARSKViewDelegate 273
Adding a spawn point 273
Handling problems with the AR session 275
Key points 278

Chapter 14: Raycasting & Physics 279
Spawning emojis 280
Enabling physics 282
Force 285
Torque 287
Actions 289
Understanding 2D raycasting 294
Handling touches 295
Adding finishing touches 296
Key points 297

Section VI: ARKit & SceneKit 299

Chapter 15: ARKit & SceneKit 301
What is SceneKit? 302
Creating a SceneKit AR project 302
Exploring the project 304
Loading & exploring the Starter project 307
App state management 309
Basic scene management 310
AR session management 313
AR Coaching Overlay 318
Key points 322

Chapter 16: Focus Nodes & Billboards 323
Importing 3D assets 323
Focus nodes 325
Adding billboard constraints 330

Creating the scene 334
Adding a shadow catcher 338
Loading the scene 339
Presenting the scene 340
Adding interaction 341
Enabling statistics & debugging (optional) 344
Adding the final touches 345
Key points 347

Section VII: ECS & Collaborative Experiences (Bonus Section) 349

Chapter 17: ECS & Collaborative Experiences 351
Exploring the project 352
Creating the AR View 354
What is ECS? 356
Creating the game board 357
Placing content 361
Collaborative experiences 365
Configuring RealityKit for collaboration 369
Requesting network permissions 371
Managing ownership 372
Removing anchors 373
Key points 375

Conclusion 377

Book License

By purchasing *Apple Augmented Reality by Tutorials*, you have the following license:

- You are allowed to use and/or modify the source code in *Apple Augmented Reality by Tutorials* in as many apps as you want, with no attribution required.

- You are allowed to use and/or modify all art, images and designs that are included in *Apple Augmented Reality by Tutorials* in as many apps as you want, but must include this attribution line somewhere inside your app: "Artwork/images/designs: from *Apple Augmented Reality by Tutorials*, available at www.raywenderlich.com".

- The source code included in *Apple Augmented Reality by Tutorials* is for your personal use only. You are NOT allowed to distribute or sell the source code in *Apple Augmented Reality by Tutorials* without prior authorization.

- This book is for your personal use only. You are NOT allowed to sell this book without prior authorization, or distribute it to friends, coworkers or students; they would need to purchase their own copies.

All materials provided with this book are provided on an "as is" basis, without warranty of any kind, express or implied, including but not limited to the warranties of merchantability, fitness for a particular purpose and noninfringement. In no event shall the authors or copyright holders be liable for any claim, damages or other liability, whether in an action of contract, tort or otherwise, arising from, out of or in connection with the software or the use or other dealings in the software.

All trademarks and registered trademarks appearing in this guide are the properties of their respective owners.

Before You Begin

This section tells you a few things you need to know before you get started, such as what you'll need for hardware and software, where to find the project files for this book, and more.

What You Need

To follow along with this book, you'll need the following:

- A Mac running **macOS Catalina** (10.15) or later. Earlier versions might work, but they're untested.

- **Xcode 11 or later**. Xcode is the main development tool for iOS. You'll need Xcode 11 or later to complete the projects in this book. You can download the latest version of Xcode from Apple's developer site here: apple.co/2asi58y

- An **AR-capable iOS device with iOS 13 or later** installed. Any iOS device with an A9 chip or newer that has iOS 11 or newer installed will support AR. However, the latest features, such as motion capture and people occlusion, will only run on a device with an A12 Bionic processor or newer and iOS 13 or newer.

If you haven't installed the latest version of macOS and Xcode, be sure to do so before continuing with the book.

Book Source Code & Forums

Where to download the materials for this book

The materials for this book can be cloned or downloaded from the GitHub book materials repository:

- https://github.com/raywenderlich/apr-materials/tree/editions/1.0

Forums

We've also set up an official forum for the book at https://forums.raywenderlich.com/c/books/apple-augmented-reality-by-tutorials. This is a great place to ask questions about the book or to submit any errors you may find.

Introduction

Welcome to your first step into Apple's wonderful world of augmented reality (AR).

This book is the easiest and fastest way to get hands-on experience using Apple frameworks and technologies like Reality Composer, RealityKit, and ARKit — all the available rendering technologies Apple has to offer, as well as a collection of fun projects for creating various real-world AR experiences.

After reading this book, you'll have a deep understanding of the technologies and frameworks used to create powerful, immersive AR experiences for the Apple platform.

How to read this book

To get the most out of this book, you should read the pages in the order they are presented.

This book is split into seven main sections:

Section I: Reality Composer

In this section, you'll dip your toes into the shallow end of augmented reality as you learn about AR Quick Look, Reality Composer, Reality and USDZ Files. You'll create an interactive virtual drum kit that you'll be able to share with your friends on iMessage.

Section II: Reality Composer & Image Tracking

In this section, you'll dive a little deeper into augmented reality and learn about image anchors and tracking. You'll also create an interactive AR Business Card that you can show off to your friends, making them green with envy.

Section III: Reality Composer & Object Tracking

In this section, you'll add another dimension with Object tracking. Using object anchors, you'll augment a physical toy truck with interactive buttons that will reveal some fun facts about its real-world counterpart.

Section IV: RealityKit & Face Tracking

In this section, you'll learn about RealityKit and face tracking. You'll create a SnapChat-like face filter app with SwiftUI that lets you mockup your face with funny props. You'll also create an animated mask that you can control with your eyes, brows and mouth.

Section V: ARKit & SpriteKit

In this section, you'll get a full introduction to ARKit and find out what makes it so powerful. In doing so, you'll create a fun 2D SpriteKit game where you get to save tiny Emoji's before they fall to their death.

Section VI: ARKit & SceneKit

In this section, you'll continue learning about ARKit. You'll also learn about SceneKit, Apple's framework for creating 3D content, as you build a miniature interactive virtual airport that allows customers to access basic departure and arrivals information.

Section VII: ECS & Collaborative Experiences (Bonus Section)

In this section, you'll create a multiplayer AR shared experience using RealityKit. In this experience, two players can play a basic Knots & Crosses game on separate devices.

Section I: Reality Composer

Welcome to the first section of the book. In this section, you'll dip your toes into the shallow end of augmented reality as you learn about AR Quick Look, Reality Composer, Reality and USDZ Files. You'll create an interactive virtual drum kit that you'll be able to share with your friends on iMessage.

Chapter 1: AR Quick Start

Welcome to your first step into Apple's wonderful world of augmented reality (AR)!

This chapter has been designed from the ground up to satisfy the need to create an Augmented Reality App with Xcode as quickly — and impatiently — as possible. Who wants to read pages upon pages of information before getting to the fun part? Well, you're in luck, because the fun begins right now!

In this chapter, you'll create a fun little augmented reality app using Xcode. By the end of this chapter, you'll have a fully remote-controllable Tiny Toy Tank. You'll be able to drive it around and make it aim and shoot at stuff. Sound good? Great! It's time to get to it.

Augmented
Reality App

Creating an AR project with Xcode

In the following section, you'll create a small augmented reality app project using Xcode.

Start **Xcode**, then create a new project by selecting **File ▸ New ▸ Project…**. When asked to choose a new template for your project, select **iOS ▸ Application ▸ Augmented Reality App**, then click **Next** to continue.

Enter **TinyToyTank** for the **Product Name** and choose **RealityKit** as your **Content Technology** of choice.

Make sure to set the **Interface** to **Storyboard** before clicking **Next** to continue.

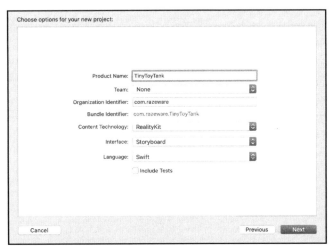

Select a secure location to save your project. To keep things simple, the **Desktop** is always a good place. Once that's done, click **Create** to finalize the project creation process.

Excellent, you've just created an augmented reality app with Xcode. Congratulations, chapter done! :]

Wait, didn't someone mention something about a Tiny Toy Tank? Oh, of course, yes, continue on, then.

> **Note**: Feel free to do a quick build and run at this point. You'll see a glorious cube sitting on the nearest flat surface in front of you. How boring! Now, if that was a pretty-looking tank, it would be much more interesting.

Exploring the project

Not to spend too much time on this, but take a look at some of the key components Xcode generated for your augmented reality app:

- **AppDelegate.swift**: Here's the starting point of your app.

- **ViewController.swift**: All of the code behind the entire AR experience resides here. You'll add a lot more code to this file, too.

- **Experience.rcproject**: This is a Reality Composer project. It contains all of the 3D assets, animations and sounds you'll use for the AR experience. You'll replace it with a custom project containing all of the graphics, animations and sound effects for the Tiny Toy Tank AR experience.

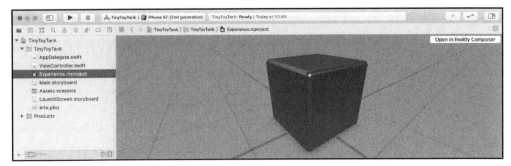

- **Assets.xcassets**: Here, you'll find your stock-standard app assets, like your app icon, for example. You'll add some images for the buttons here.

- **Main.storyboard**: Contains all of the UI for your app. You'll add some basic control buttons for the Tiny Toy Tank here.

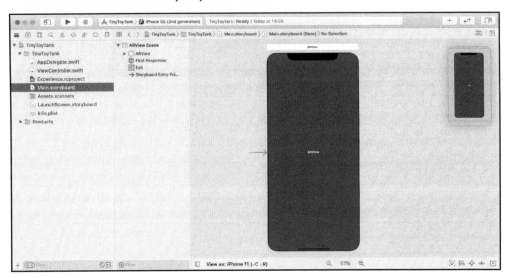

- **Info.plist**: This one is important when dealing with AR apps. It's where your app requests access to various hardware components, like the camera, for example, to deliver the AR experience.

Great, a lot of stuff is ready for you out of the box. Now that you're aware of what's contained within the default project template, you can start adding some custom content.

Asking for camera permission

To present an AR experience, the user must grant your app access to the device camera. You do this by adding the **Privacy — Camera Usage Description** property to **Info.plist**. Your **Info.plist** already has this property, but it still needs a proper description.

With **Info.plist** open, set the value of **Privacy — Camera Usage Description** to **AR experience requires access to Camera**.

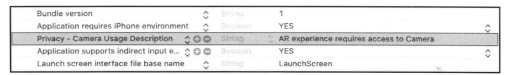

Now, when your app launches, it'll request access to the camera, explaining to the user that it needs that access to deliver the AR experience.

Adding custom assets

All of the 3D assets that the Tiny Toy Tank experience requires are contained within a single Reality Composer project file. You're going to add it to your project now.

Using Finder, locate **starter/resources/TinyToyTank/TinyToyTank.rcproject**. Drag and drop this file into your project, placing it immediately below **Experience.rcproject**.

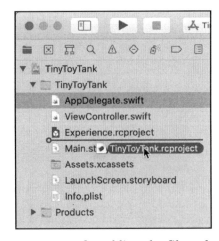

When prompted to choose an option for adding the file, select **Copy items if needed** to add a copy of the file, not a reference, to your project. Select **Finish** to complete the process.

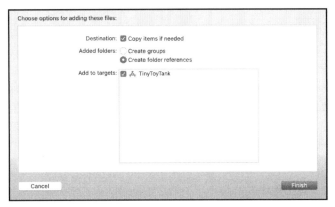

Select **TinyToyTank.rcproject** in the project hierarchy and meet the hero of your AR app — the glorious **Tiny Toy Tank**.

Exploring the Reality Composer project

You might wonder what's inside this **Reality Composer** project file. To take a closer look, select the **Open in Reality Composer** button at the top-right of the view. The project will open up in Reality Composer, a companion app that's installed with Xcode.

In the top bar, select **Scenes** to view the **Scenes** panel and select **Properties** to see the current scene's properties.

Note that this project only contains one scene named **TinyToyTank** and that it uses a **Horizontal** anchor type.

Select the **Behaviors** option to reveal the Behaviors panel at the bottom.

Here, you'll find a collection of **Behaviors**, which animate the tank and play sound effects. Select the **TurretLeft** behavior, then select the little **Play** button next to the **Action Sequence**.

The turret on top of the tank will turn left while making a ratchet sound. When it's done, the turret resets to its original position. You'll use all of these behaviors to move and turn the tank.

Enough about that for now, you'll learn more about Reality Composer and its features in another chapter. For now, close Reality Composer and jump back into Xcode.

Presenting the custom scene

Currently, the AR experience is only showing a box. You need to change it to show the tank instead.

Open **ViewController.swift** so you can make some code changes.

Declare the following variable at the top of `ViewController`:

```
var tankAnchor: TinyToyTank._TinyToyTank?
```

This declares **tankAnchor** as type **_TinyToyTank**, which you'll initialize by loading the **TinyToyTank** scene from the **Reality Composer** project.

Replace the contents of `viewDidLoad()` with:

```
// 1
super.viewDidLoad()
// 2
tankAnchor = try! TinyToyTank.load_TinyToyTank()
// 3
arView.scene.anchors.append(tankAnchor!)
```

Look at what's happening here:

1. This ensures that the super class `viewDidLoad()` is called.

2. Xcode has generated access methods to the **TinyToyTank.rcproject**. Here, you're using `load_TinyToyTank()` to load the scene and store it in **tankAnchor**.

Excellent, now you're presenting the newly-added **TinyTankScene** instead of the old **Box** scene from **Experience.rcproject**.

To keep your project nicely organized and clean, now would be a great time to remove **Experience.rcproject** from your project. Right-click it then select **Delete**. When asked, select **Move to Trash** to completely remove it.

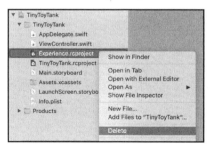

Now that you've removed the file, your project is once again clean and organized. It's time to test things out. Connect your device, then build and run.

Your app starts and requests permission to access the camera. Once you grant that permission, point the camera toward a flat surface. A tiny tank will spawn out of thin air, placing itself right on top of that surface. Amazing!

It's a pretty little tank indeed, but it ain't moving? That's no fun! You'll take care of that next.

Setting up the UI

You'll need to add some on-screen controls for the user to let them control the tank. There are a several button images for you to use under **starter/resources/Buttons**.

Select **Assets.scnassets** then drag and drop all of the images into it.

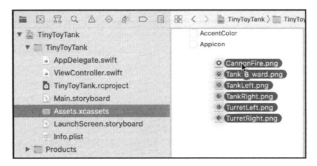

Setting up ARView

Now that you've added the images, you need to configure the UI. Keep in mind, this chapter is not about building UIs, it's about creating the AR experience. With that in mind, and to keep things as simple as possible, you're going to take some shortcuts when creating the UI.

Open **Main.storyboard**, then select **ARView Scene ▸ ARView ▸ Ar View**.

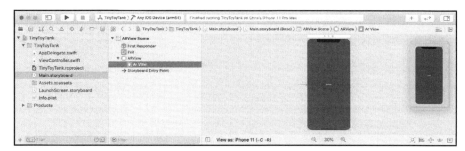

Press **Backspace** to delete it. You can't use the current **ARView** alone as a container for other UI elements; you have to use an **UIView** instead.

Open **Object Library** by selecting the + sign at the top, then search for the **UIView**. Drag and drop it onto the **ARView** view controller.

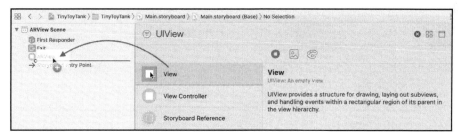

Open the **Object Library** again, then search for **ARView**. Drag and drop a **RealityKit AR View** into the design view.

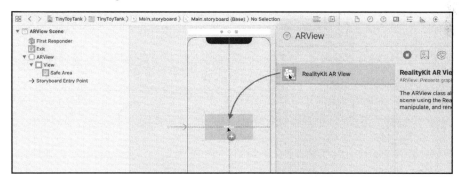

Manually adjust the control points so that it fits over the entire screen. Then, under the **Size Inspector**, turn on both **horizontal** and **vertical Autoresizing**. This will keep the **ARView** full screen at all times.

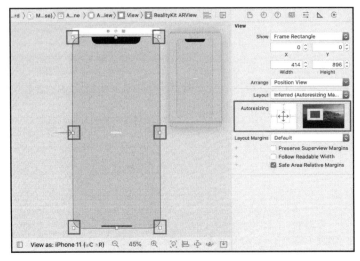

Because you recreated the **ARView** from scratch, you need to reconnect it to the `arView` outlet in **ViewController.swift**.

Create a side-by-side view so that you can see **Main.storyboard** on one side and **ViewController.swift** on the other.

From the view controller side, click, drag and connect the `arView` outlet to **RealityKit ARView**.

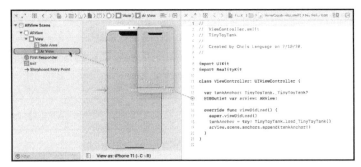

The view will rename itself: **Ar View**.

Finally, you're ready to add the buttons.

Adding buttons

Open the **Object Library** and search for **Button**. Drag and drop a **Button** into the design view.

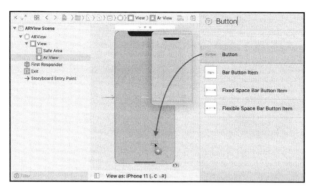

Rename the button **TankRight**, then under the **Attributes Inspector**, select the **TankRight** image for it.

Under the **Size inspector**, set the **Width** and **Height** to 80. Under **Autoresizing**, anchor the button to the **Bottom-Right**.

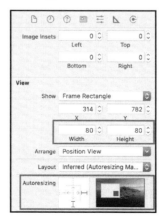

Finally, move the button to the bottom-right of the design view.

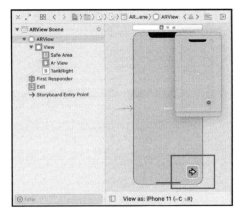

Go into a side-by-side view and open **ViewController.swift** next to **Main.storyboard**. While holding down **Control**, click and drag from the **TankRight** button into the view controller.

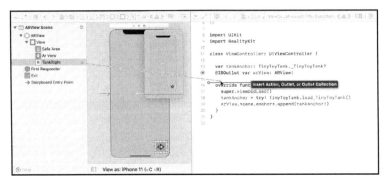

Insert an **Action** named **tankRightPressed**. Select **Connect** to complete the new connection.

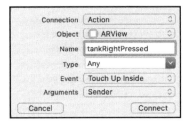

Once you're done, you'll see the newly-created `@IBAction`.

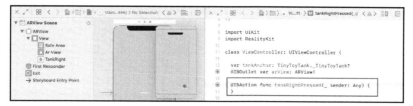

Now, when the user presses the **TankRight** button, it will trigger `tankRightPressed()` within the `ViewController`.

Follow the same steps as above and add the remaining buttons. Here's a list of the remaining buttons.

Button Name	Image	Action Outlet
TankForward	TankForward	tankForwardPressed
TankLeft	TankLeft	tankLeftPressed
TurretRight	TurrentRight	turretRightPressed
CannonFire	CannonFire	cannonFirePressed
TurretLeft	TurretLeft	turretLeftPressed

The final result should look like this:

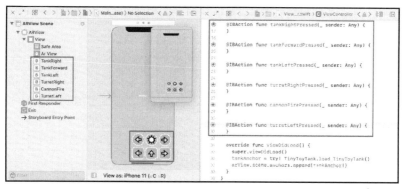

All six buttons are connected to their outlets in the `ViewController`. Congratulations, you've finished the UI.

Adding tank animations

Now that the UI is set, you need to make the tank move on command. To do that, you only need to invoke those behaviors you saw earlier, within the Reality Composer project.

Start with the tank movement. Add the following line to `tankRightPressed(_:)`:

```
tankAnchor!.notifications.tankRight.post()
```

You can access any of the available behaviors through `notifications`. You invoke them by calling `post()` on the behavior.

Continue to add the other behaviors.

Add the following line of code to `tankForwardPressed(_:)`:

```
tankAnchor!.notifications.tankForward.post()
```

And this code to `tankLeftPressed(_:)`:

```
tankAnchor!.notifications.tankLeft.post()
```

Build and run to test it out.

Great, the tank moves when you press forward, left and right. But hang on, something is horribly wrong. The turret on top of the tank isn't moving with it. What's going on here?

Parenting entities

The problem you're experiencing is the fact that the turret is currently a separate entity — it's not connected to the tank. To connect the turret to the tank, you need to set the tank as the turret's parent. That way, when the tank entity moves and rotates, its child entities will move and rotate with it.

Add the following line of code to `viewDidLoad()`, right after `tankAnchor` has been initialized:

```
tankAnchor!.turret?.setParent(
  tankAnchor!.tank, preservingWorldTransform: true)
```

This sets the **tank** entity as the **turret** entity's parent. Preserving the **World Transform** while parenting the tank to the turret keeps the current position of the turret relative to the tank's current position, as you see it in the scene.

Build and run again, and you'll see you've attached the turret nicely to the tank.

Adding turret animations

Finally, you can now continue to add the turret behaviors to rotate it left and right — and don't forget the all-important behavior to fire the gun.

Add the following line of code to `turretRightPressed(_:)`:

```
tankAnchor!.notifications.turretRight.post()
```

Then, add the following to `turretLeftPressed(_:)`:

```
tankAnchor!.notifications.turretLeft.post()
```

And to make the cannon fire, add the following line of code to `cannonFirePressed(_:)`:

```
tankAnchor!.notifications.cannonFire.post()
```

That's it, you now have full control over your tank. Build and run again to test it.

The tank moves on command, the turret stays connected to the tank and moves with it. The turret moves independently from the tank and fires off its cannon like a champ. But hang on, there's yet another issue.

Final touches

When the user's a bit trigger happy and presses the button too enthusiastically, the animation goes pear-shaped. When pressing a button while an animation is playing, the next animation is compounded on top of the currently-playing animation, which has some undesired side effects. This could lead to the turret being stuck in mid-air, for example.

The best way to solve this issue is to prevent any other animations from playing while an animation is currently active.

Add the following declaration to the top of `ViewController`:

```
var isActionPlaying: Bool = false
```

When an animation triggers, you'll set `isActionPlaying` to `true`. Then, while it's `true`, you can prevent any other animations from triggering.

To do this, add the following code to the top of all of the "button pressed event" handlers:

```
if self.isActionPlaying { return }
else { self.isActionPlaying = true }
```

Now, when the user presses a button to kick off an animation, it will first check to see if there's an animation already in progress. If there is, it will ignore the button press. If not, it will set the flag to indicate that there is now an animation in progress, right before kicking of the actual animation.

You still need to reset `isActionPlaying` once the animation completes. To solve that, the behaviors have already been configured to send back a notification once the animation sequence completes. You just need to react to it.

Add the following code to `viewDidLoad()`, right after setting the tank as the turret's parent:

```
tankAnchor?.actions.actionComplete.onAction = { _ in
    self.isActionPlaying = false
}
```

Each behavior will send an **actionComplete** notification once its animation sequence ends. Here, you're creating a little handler that makes sure `isActionPlaying` resets to `false`, which allows another animation to play.

That's it, you're done. Build and run one last time and test out the glorious Tiny Toy Tank.

Now would be a good time to look away, because the little bear is about to get it! :]

> **Note**: For completeness' sake, there are a bunch of app icons you can use under **starter/resources/AppIcons**. Just drag and drop them into the **AppIcon** component of **Assets.xcassets**.

You can find a copy of the final project under the **final/TinyToyTank** folder.

Key points

Congratulations on finishing this chapter. You now know how quick and easy it is to create an AR experience with Xcode.

Take a look at some of the key points you picked up along the way:

- **Xcode AR Templates**: It's super easy to create an AR experience with Xcode. It comes with a collection of AR templates out of the box, giving you a quick starting point for your AR projects.

- **User Interface**: You learned how to create a very basic user interface allowing the user to interact with the AR content. You can easily extend this with touch-based gestures or even voice activation for more intuitive interaction. Later, you'll also learn how to create a SwiftUI-based UI.

- **Reality Composer**: In this project, you got a quick introduction to Reality Composer. You'll learn more about using this extremely powerful tool in the coming chapters.

- **RealityKit**: You got a real quick introduction to RealityKit. Now, you shouldn't be intimidated by the coding component of creating AR experiences. In the coming chapters, you'll learn more about it with a few more project examples.

- **3D Virtual Content**: In this chapter, you used ready-made 3D virtual content, but that won't be the case when you're working on your own projects from scratch. In the coming chapters, you'll learn much more about content creation, which is an extremely important part of creating AR experiences.

Go take your Tiny Toy Tank for a spin and shoot at a few things. See you soon in the next chapter.

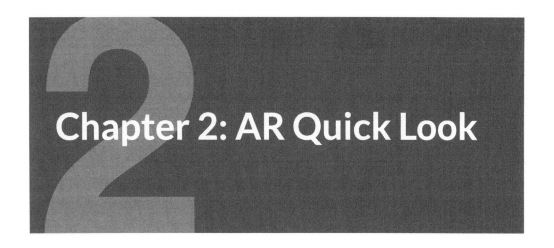

Chapter 2: AR Quick Look

The message from Apple is crystal clear: Augmented reality (AR) is here to stay, and it's going to play a big part in the future of the iPhone. Ever since the release of ARKit 2.0 and iOS 12 at WWDC 2018, Apple has deeply integrated AR into the core of all its operating systems.

Even apps like iMessage, Mail, Notes, News, Safari and Files now have support for AR.

This is thanks to **AR Quick Look**, which is the simplest way to present AR content on mobile devices. In this chapter, you'll learn about AR Quick Look. You'll see how easy it is to integrate it into your own apps to give them some cool AR superpowers.

What is AR Quick Look?

You're probably already familiar with **Quick Look**, which lets you quickly peek at images, PDFs and spreadsheets in apps like Mail and Safari. Quick Look is a framework that does the heavy lifting for you, giving your app superpowers that let it support a wide selection of universal file formats.

Here's the best part: Quick Look now offers support for **USDZ** and **Reality** file formats via its **AR Quick Look** feature.

AR Quick Look lets you showcase a virtual 3D model of a physical product within your local space. The model appears grounded in your environment, giving you a good sense of how the physical product looks.

Imagine you want to buy a new sofa. A shopping app with this technology lets you check out how various sofas actually look in your living room.

AR Quick Look achieves a high degree of realism by mimicking realistic lighting conditions in your local environment. It combines this lighting with soft shadows and physically-based rendering (PBR) materials that shine and reflect the local environment, just like the real thing.

Using AR Quick Look is as simple as providing it with the path to your USDZ or Reality content and letting it do its magic. And there are lots of nifty things you can do with it, too.

AR Quick Look features

At face value, AR Quick Look seems simple enough. When you dig deeper, however, you'll notice that it comes with a bucket-load of insanely cool features.

Here's a look at what's inside:

- **Anchors**: Anchors allow you to anchor virtual content to various real-world surfaces. With the release of iOS 13, AR Quick Look supports horizontal surfaces like floors, ceilings, tables and chairs; vertical surfaces like walls; images including photos and posters; and faces and objects like toys and consumer products.

- **Occlusion**: Occlusion allows the physical world to obscure virtual content based on its depth relative to the real world. AR Quick Look currently offers occlusion for people and faces. This feature works only on certain devices.

- **Physics, Forces and Collisions**: Virtual content responds to the laws of physics. Objects can fall due to gravity and bounce and collide with one another.

- **Triggers and Behaviors**: Users can reach into AR and interact with objects to trigger events, animations and sounds.

- **Realtime Shadows**: Virtual content casts realistic-looking shadows onto real-world surfaces. The quality of the shadows depends on the device's capabilities. Low-end devices project shadows, while high-end devices use ray-traced shadows.

- **High Dynamic Range, Tone Mapping and Color Correction**: AR Quick Look samples the local environment in real time and uses the results to control the virtual content's brightness, color and tone. This makes objects seem to blend naturally with their surroundings.

- **Camera Grain, Motion Blur and Depth of Field**: Post-processing camera effects push the visual fidelity to the next level. Fast-moving objects blur, distant objects appear out of focus and adding a grain effect to crisp-looking virtual content makes it blend in with a typical grainy camera feed.

- **Multi-Sampling and Specular Anti-aliasing**: AR Quick Look anti-aliases the virtual content's edges to smooth out pixelation. It also anti-aliases specular reflections to prevent flickering.

- **Physically Based Rendering Clear Coat Materials**: Apply super-realistic materials to virtual content so your objects look exactly like their real-life counterparts.

- **Ambient and Spatial Audio**: Ambient sounds add another level of realism to virtual content. Objects produce spatially-accurate sound effects based on their location in physical space and their position relative to the camera.

- **Integration and Customization**: You can easily integrate AR Quick Look into Web, iOS, macOS and tvOS apps.

- **Apple Pay**: Apple Pay is fully integrated into AR Quick Look. Users can impulse buy your products without leaving the AR experience.

As you can see, AR Quick Look gives you the flexibility to make your products shine in AR. However, there are a few limitations to keep in mind while you work with it.

AR Quick Look limitations

Although AR Quick Look offers plenty of features, it's important to note that the AR experience scales back some effects based on the capabilities of the user's device. Only the latest and greatest high-end devices are capable of offering the full experience.

This might seem obvious, but it's worth mentioning that AR Quick Look is only available in the Apple ecosystem. You can't view AR Quick Look content on devices that run Android, Windows or any other non-Apple operating system.

AR Quick Look experiences are also somewhat limited due to the lack of any kind of scriptable or codable pipeline. More intelligent AR experiences require you to create apps for them.

Experiencing AR Quick Look

Apple offers a fantastic gallery of 3D models that you can use to explore AR Quick Look. If you're running iOS 12 or newer on a device, you can try it for yourself.

Open the following link in Safari: https://apple.co/2C5362d

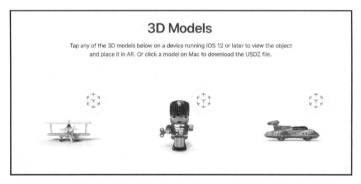

These models use the USDZ format, and thanks to AR Quick Look, Safari now has built-in support for that format.

Did you notice that tiny cube on each of the model images?

That's Apple's signature icon to indicate that the model is viewable in AR.

So, what are you waiting for? Pick an option and try it for yourself.

AR mode

When you pick a model, Safari launches AR Quick Look, which loads the referenced USDZ file from a URL and presents it to you.

It launches directly into AR mode to get the user into AR as quickly as possible.

Wait, what the duck! Is that Launchpad McQuack?

As soon as AR Quick Look detects the desired surface, it automatically places the 3D model on top of that surface. The experience is seamless and, with quality virtual content, you can easily believe you're seeing the real thing.

There are a few things you can do while in AR mode:

- **Positioning**: You can easily position the 3D model with a tap, hold and drag gesture to place the model wherever you want. AR Quick Look understands both horizontal and vertical surfaces. So if there's a wall behind the model, you can simply drag the model onto the wall, and it'll stick.
- **Scaling**: Scale the 3D model larger or smaller with a pinch-in or -out gesture. Reset the scale to 100% by double-tapping the 3D model.
- **Rotating**: Rotate the 3D model by placing two fingers on the screen and moving them in a circular motion. Again, a double-tap gesture will reset the rotation.
- **Levitating**: Defy gravity and levitate the 3D model with a two-finger upwards-drag gesture.
- **Snapshots**: Take cool pictures of your AR experience by quickly tapping the camera shutter button once. This will save a snapshot to your photos.
- **Videos**: You can even make a video recording of your AR experience by holding down the camera shutter button for a short time. As soon as you let go, AR Quick Look will automatically save the video clip to your photos. Excellent!
- **Sharing**: Select the share button at the top-right and you'll get a list of apps that let you share the current model. How about AirDropping it to a nearby friend?

Share button options:

Once you're done playing, you can close AR Quick Look with the **X** button at the top-left corner. You'll return to the webpage, where you can explore some of the other cool 3D models.

Object mode

Switch into **Object mode** by selecting the **Object** tab in AR mode. Here, you can inspect the 3D model with the same basic gestures to manipulate it, like pinch to scale and swipe to rotate.

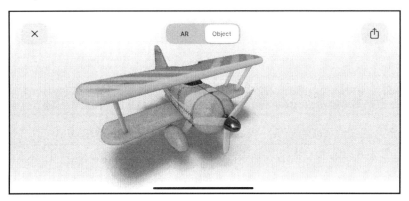

With Object mode, you're able to see the object's details without the distractions of the real world around it.

Once you've finished looking at the models, you're ready to move on to learning how to add augmented reality to your websites.

AR Quick Look for web

As of iOS 12, Safari has built-in support for previewing USDZ and Reality files, thanks to AR Quick Look. In this section, you'll learn how to integrate USDZ file support into your own websites.

Open the **starter_web** folder and double-click **index.html**. This launches Safari and loads the following web page:

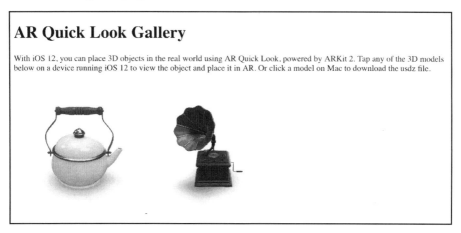

This is an example web page with two USDZ models. When you inspect the files in the folder, you'll observe three images along with three USDZ files.

Your next step is to go through the process of adding another USDZ model to your AR gallery.

Open **index.html** using a plain text editor.

> **Note**: To edit HTML files, you need to use a plain text editor; TextEdit tends to render the file rather than give you access to the underlying HTML code. If you do not have a plain text editor, you can use Xcode to edit the file.

Add the following HTML markup to the bottom of the file, just above the </body> tag:

```
<a href="pig.usdz" rel="ar">
</a>
```

This adds a standard <a> tag, which creates references to URLs. Look at the provided attributes:

- **href**: This is set to **pig.usdz**. It points to the USDZ file that you're referencing, which is in the same location as **index.html**.

- **rel**: This attribute specifies the relationship between the current document and the linked document. In this case, you're setting the relationship to **ar**, indicating that the referenced document is an AR model.

Now, add the following line of code just before the previously-added </a> tag:

```
<img src="pig.jpg" width="250" height="250">
```

Up to this point, the reference to the USDZ file was invisible on the webpage. This line of code adds an image to the reference, giving the user something to tap.

Finally, open **.htaccess** with a text editor and add the following line:

```
AddType model/vnd.usdz+zip .usdz
```

This adds the required MIME type so Safari knows what to do with the USDZ file type.

> **Note**: To support Reality files, use the following MIME type:
>
> AddType model/vnd.reality .reality

Save your changes and test. Once again, open **index.html** in Safari.

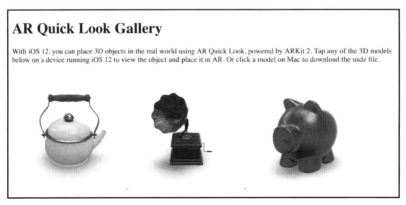

That's it; you just added another USDZ file to your webpage. Fantastic!

> **Note**: You can only experience AR Quick Look on an actual device running iOS 12 or newer. You also need to deploy your webpage to an actual web server to browse to it from your device. Setting up a local web server falls outside the scope of this book.

If you're wondering how to add **AR Quick View** support to existing apps, you've come to the right place. You're going to do that next.

AR Quick Look for apps

Your first step to add AR Quick Look to an app is to open the starter project from the **starter** folder. It's a basic single-view app with a `UITableView` and a custom cell that shows a small image and a name.

Do a quick build and run to test it.

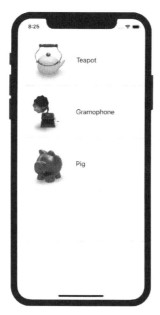

When you select a row, nothing happens yet. All you're doing at this point is storing the selected row index in a variable named `modelIndex`. You'll use this variable later.

Next, you'll load the images using an array of strings named `modelNames`, which links directly to the images stored in **Assets.xcassets**.

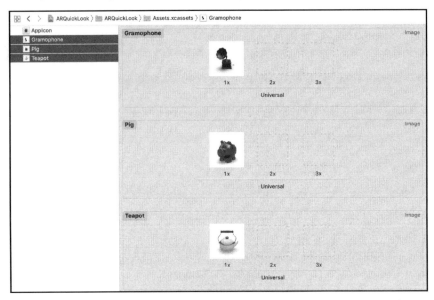

Import the USDZ files into the project by dragging and dropping the **Models** folder, found inside **resources**, into the project.

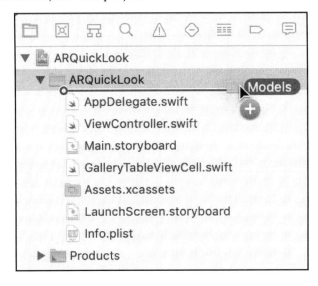

Make sure you've checked **Add to targets**, then click **Finish** to complete the process.

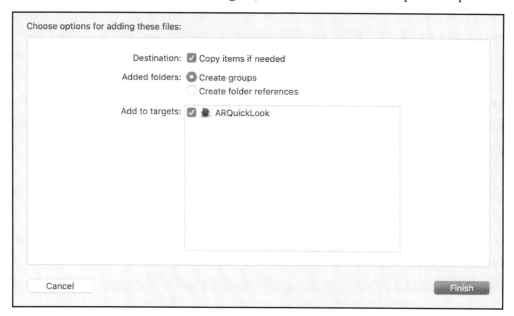

You'll now see a new **Models** group inside the project; you can preview the USDZ files within Xcode.

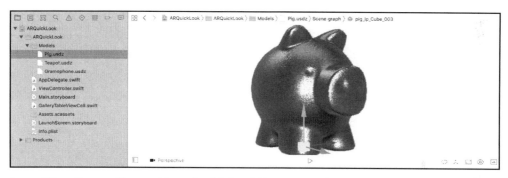

Open **ViewController.swift** and add the following to the top of the file:

```
import QuickLook
```

This imports the **QuickLook** framework, which is required to implement the AR Quick Look functionality within your app.

Next, add the following protocols to `ViewController`:

```
QLPreviewControllerDelegate, QLPreviewControllerDataSource
```

Here's a closer look at these protocols:

- **QLPreviewControllerDelegate**: This protocol lets the preview controller provide a zoom animation for the Quick Look preview. It also specifies if your app opens a URL and responds to the opening and closing of the preview.

- **QLPreviewControllerDataSource**: This protocol lets the data source tell the QLPreviewController how many items to include in a preview item navigation list.

Implement the protocols by adding the following below QLPreviewControllerDataSource:

```
func numberOfPreviewItems(in controller: QLPreviewController) ->
Int {
  return 1
}
```

When previewing AR content, you're *always* going to preview only one object at a time. So when the data source queries the number of preview items, you tell it that there's only one item available for preview.

Add the following function below the previously-added function:

```
func previewController(
  _ controller: QLPreviewController,
  previewItemAt index: Int) -> QLPreviewItem {
  let url = Bundle.main.url(
    forResource: modelNames[modelIndex],
    withExtension: "usdz")!
  return url as QLPreviewItem
}
```

So what's going on in the code above? When the preview controller requests the resourceURL, you construct the URL for the selected resource name at modelIndex in the modelNames array. You also specify the resource extension as **usdz**. Finally, the code passes the URL back to the controller as a QLPreviewItem.

You've now implemented all the Quick Look protocols. The only thing left to do is present the preview.

Add the following lines of code to the bottom of tableView(_:didSelectRowAt:):

```
// 1
let previewController = QLPreviewController()
// 2
previewController.dataSource = self
```

```
previewController.delegate = self
// 3
present(previewController, animated: false)
```

Finally, you're ready to present the AR Quick Look preview to the user. With this code:

1. You create an instance of `QLPreviewController`.

2. Next, you nominate the `ViewController` class as `dataSource` and `delegate` for the preview controller.

3. Finally, you present the preview controller to the user.

That's it, you're done! Your app can use AR Quick Look now. Build and run to test it.

> **Note**: Make sure your device is running iOS 12 or newer, or you won't be able to see it.

You're about to witness Uncle Scrooge banking a coin!

Key points

Well done, you've reached the end of the first chapter.

Here's what you learned:

- Apple has deeply integrated AR into iOS, macOS and tvOS. Many commonly-used apps provide AR support with AR Quick Look.

- AR Quick Look is feature rich and provides a premier augmented reality experience out of the box. Users instinctively know what to do.

- AR Quick Look uses USDZ and Reality files.

- You can use USDZ and Reality content on the web. Upload your file and create a stock-standard reference to it. Thanks to its built-in support, Safari's smart enough to know it can view the content with AR Quick Look. It automatically gives the user that mind-blowing AR experience.

- Need to add AR support to some of your existing apps? AR Quick Look has your back. Simply add your USDZ and Reality files to your existing project along with some sampled images. Then use `QLPreviewController` to do the heavy lifting for you.

Where to go from here?

Here are a few links to expand your knowledge on this topic:

- **Quick Look Documentation**: https://apple.co/2JQ9mN7

- **Quick Look at WWDC 2019**: https://apple.co/32NPqSd

Now that you know all there is to know about AR Quick Look, you might wonder how you create your own USDZ and Reality files. Well, continue to the next chapter to find out!

Chapter 3: Reality Composer & Reality Files

Now that you know all about AR Quick Look, it's time to dip your toes a little deeper into the shallow end of Augmented Reality (AR). In this chapter, you'll learn about Reality Composer and Reality Files.

Until recently, creating immersive AR experiences was a somewhat difficult task. AR developers required a vast amount of skill, as well as knowledge of a wide variety of technologies, just to make a little cube appear in AR. That all changed when Apple announced **Reality Composer**.

Reality Composer

What is Reality Composer?

Reality Composer is an AR authoring tool that lets you create interactive AR-based experiences with an intuitive WYSIWYG (What You See Is What You Get) design. It's self-explanatory and super easy to use. You don't need any prior coding or 3D development experience to use it.

Any AR Quick Look-compatible app, including iMessage, Safari, Files and even apps you build yourself, can then view the AR experiences you create.

Reality Composer is fully integrated into Xcode, which allows you to easily extend and customize your app's AR experiences with the power of Xcode and Swift.

If you're using an iPhone or iPad, you can download and install Reality Composer directly from the App Store using this link: **https://apple.co/2RfDvt3**

Reality Composer on an iPhone:

Although the interface is extremely compact, the app itself is fully functional, keeping you productive while you're on the go. The best part of using an iPhone is that it allows you to edit your 3D scenes directly in AR space. You experience the end result first hand – no more playing in the dark!

Reality Composer on an iPad:

The iPad's interface is similar to the iPhone's interface, but with a little more breathing room.

There's also a macOS version that installs automatically with the latest versions of Xcode.

Reality Composer on macOS:

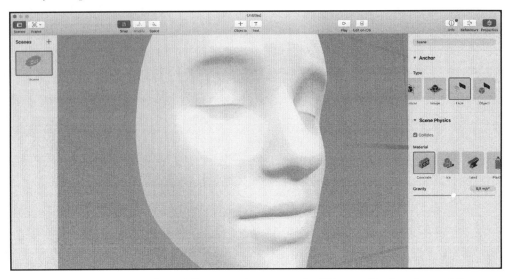

You'll notice subtle interface differences between the iPhone, iPad and macOS versions, but rest assured that the underlying functionality is exactly the same. However, the macOS version doesn't allow editing in AR space, mainly due to the lack of a rear-facing camera on most Macs.

Overall, Apple did a fantastic job at delivering an experience across multiple platforms that is consistent and pleasant.

> **Note**: At the time of writing, you can only install Reality Composer for macOS through Xcode. There's no App Store version available for download yet.

Reality Composer features

Out of the box, Reality Composer is quite impressive and includes the following features:

- **Basic Transform Editing**: With the built-in scene editor, you can easily drag, drop, rotate and scale virtual objects to construct AR scenes.

- **Edit in Augmented Space**: You can transfer scenes between macOS and iOS. This allows you to test and edit virtual scenes either on-screen or directly in augmented space.

- **Built-in Content Library**: Reality Composer comes with its own content library of virtual objects that should cover most of your AR prototyping needs. There's even a collection of primitive objects, like cubes, spheres, springs and spirals, that you can use to build your own creations.

- **USDZ File Support**: If you want a form that's not available in the built-in content library, you can create your own content and import it via a USDZ file.

- **Animations**: Bring your virtual content to life with animations that can make them wiggle and spin or put emphasis on them to attract the user's attention.

- **Spatial Audio**: You can easily add ambient sounds or special effects to your scene and virtual content. Spatial audio accurately simulates sounds emitted from objects based on their position in space.

- **Exporting**: You can either export directly to AR Quick Look or create an integrated project with Xcode where you can use code to control your virtual content.

- **Recording Sensor and Camera Data**: Pre-record sounds in an actual location, then play the recording on a simulated iOS device to test and debug the experience in Xcode. This is fantastic if you're creating an AR experience for a fixed location.

Reality Composer's limitations

Reality Composer is not perfect, and there are some limitations you need to understand before you make it your first choice for creating AR experiences. Here are a few important things to keep in mind:

- **Cross-Platform Support**: The biggest limitation you'll face is that Reality Composer restricts your AR experiences to Apple devices only. Other platforms, like Android or Windows, do not support Reality Composer.

- **iOS Support**: The latest features of AR Quick Look are only available on iOS 13 or newer. You might run into serious constraints when using a device with an older iOS version on it.

- **Scripting Support**: There's a lack of custom scripting support within AR Quick Look. If you want to create a complex AR experience, you'll have to create an Xcode app that integrates with Reality Composer instead.

> **Note**: Before you continue, make sure you've installed the latest version of Xcode. This will ensure that Reality Composer is ready to go on your Mac.
>
> You should also install Reality Composer on your iPhone or iPad, so you can test on a device later.
>
> Also, ensure that all of your devices are on the same network, which will make them discoverable.

Creating Reality Composer projects

With the basics out of the way, it's time to get those hands dirty and create your first AR experience with Reality Composer. To create a new project, all you need to do is start Reality Composer.

Use Spotlight Search to find and start the Reality Composer app that Xcode installed for you.

On start-up, Reality Composer creates a default scene for your project. Each scene has a default anchor, which forms the root position of the scene in AR space. You can anchor your AR content onto a floor, a table, a wall, an image or even a face. You'll learn more about anchors a little later.

For now, select **Horizontal** and make sure you've checked **Use template content** content. Click **Choose** to continue.

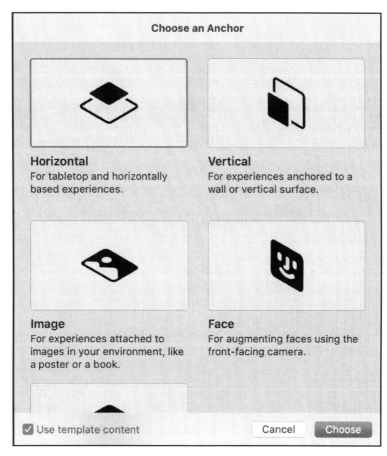

This creates the project and adds some default content. But at this point, you still haven't saved the project.

Press **Command-S** to open the **Save Project** dialog. You can also use the **File ▸ Save...** menu option to accomplish the same result.

> **Note**: It's good practice to save your project periodically, so you don't lose any progress.

Set the project name to **HelloRealityKit**, then select a more suitable destination of your choice. Select **Save** to finish.

Excellent, you've successfully created and saved your first Reality Composer project.

> **Note**: The project is available for you as a starter project under the **starter** folder. Just double-click **HelloRealityKit.rcproject** to open it in Reality Composer.

Exploring the UI

With the HelloRealityKit project open, you're ready to explore the User Interface (UI).

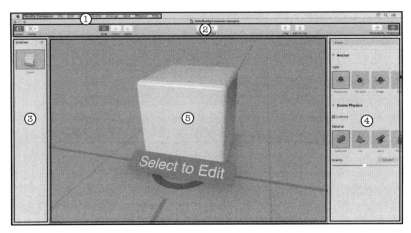

The UI consists of a few main components. Here's what each component does:

1. **Main menu**: Here, you'll find a typical menu with access to all available options.

2. **Toolbar**: The toolbar at the top of the screen contains the most commonly-used options. The shortcuts are accessible through the Main menu, but the toolbar makes them more convenient. You can customize the toolbar, so it matches your liking. Toggle its visibility by pressing **Option-Command-T**.

3. **Scenes**: The Scenes panel is on the left and provides quick access to the available scenes in the project. Simply click on the desired scene to switch to it. You can toggle its visibility by pressing **Option-Command-S**.

4. **Properties**: The Properties panel on the right shows the available attributes of the selected object. It's context-sensitive, so the properties apply to only the active selected object. Toggle its visibility by pressing **Option-Command-P**.

5. **Scene view**: The Scene view forms the center point of the UI. It's the main 3D view, where you add and manipulate virtual content and can see a live preview of your changes. You can also use the visual guides to directly transform and manipulate selected elements, changing their position, scale and rotation.

Adding scenes

Your project can contain more than one scene. Adding a new scene is as easy as clicking the + button in the top-right corner of the **Scenes** panel on the left. You could also use the Main menu by going to **Scene ▸ Add Scene...**.

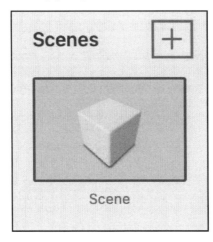

Remember that a scene is associated with an **Anchor**, so you need to choose the anchor type of the new scene.

Choose **Horizontal** again and uncheck **Use template content**. Click **Choose** to continue.

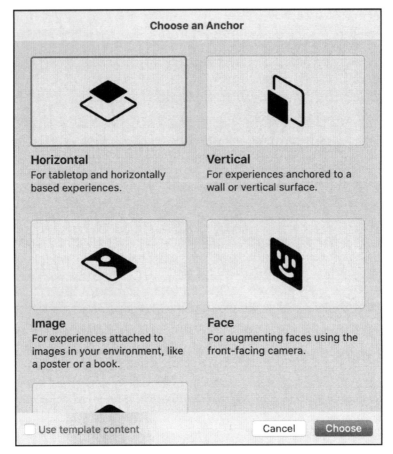

Now that you've created a new empty scene, the project contains two scenes: **Scene** and **Scene 1**. You can easily switch between the two by clicking on the scene that you want active in the Scenes panel on the right.

The contents of the Scene View will change accordingly.

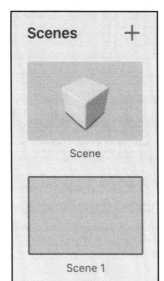

Select **Scene 1**, then continue.

Navigating scenes

To navigate around the scene, you can manipulate the view in three ways: Zoom, Pan and Rotate.

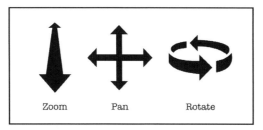

1. **Zoom**: To zoom in and out, hold down the Option key, then slide your finger backward and forward.

2. **Pan**: To pan around, slide your finger in any direction; the scene view will follow.

3. **Rotate**: To rotate the scene, press and hold the left mouse button while moving the mouse around.

> **Note**: The methods of zooming, panning and rotating mentioned above assume that you're using an Apple Magic Mouse or touchpad.

Adding objects

An empty scene isn't that exciting, so your next step is to spruce things up a bit by adding some objects to it.

Open the **Content Library** by clicking the **Objects** button with a + sign in it from the toolbar at the top of the screen.

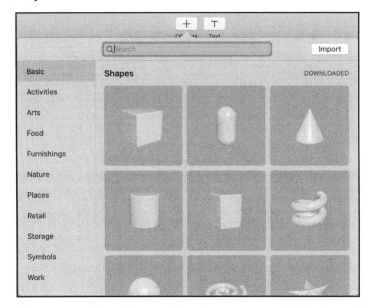

The Content Library contains a library of various shapes and 3D objects that you can use to prototype your AR scenes.

The basic shapes section is special. These are all parametric shapes, meaning that you can alter them by adjusting their parameters — more on that a little later.

Double-click the **Cube** from **Basic ▸ Shapes** to add it to the active scene.

Left-click the cube to select it.

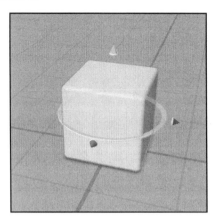

You'll notice a circle appears around the box with three colored arrows.

Each color represents a specific axis in 3D space:

- **Red**: This is the X-axis, which moves from left to right in 3D space.
- **Green**: This is the Y-axis, which goes from bottom to top in 3D space.
- **Blue**: This is the Z-axis, running from front to back in 3D space.

Right-click the cube to show contextual options.

You can easily replace, modify, cut, copy, paste, duplicate and delete objects from here. You can also use shortcut keys like backspace to delete, Command-Z to undo, Command-C to copy and Command-P to paste objects work.

Adjusting object transforms

With the 3D cube still selected, adjust its transform, which consists of three components: position, rotation and scale.

Clicking and dragging any of the arrows will move the object's position in that direction, restricting it to that selected axis.

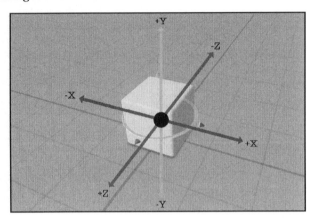

When you rotate around the scene view, the circle color will change depending on the direction you're viewing it from.

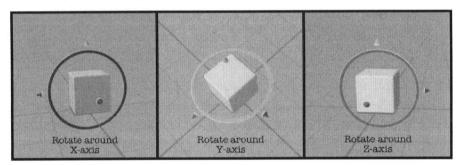

Click and drag the circle to rotate the object around the specified axis.

For more precise control over the object transform, you can adjust the settings from the Properties panel.

Adjusting object properties

With the cube still selected, open the Properties panel by clicking the **Properties** button in the toolbar.

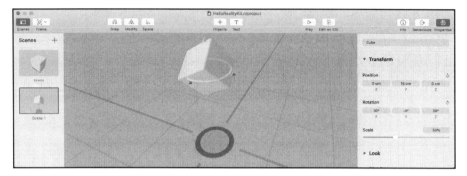

This area shows all of the available properties associated with the cube.

Change **Object Name** to **Cube**.

Expand the **Transform** section on the Properties panel, then adjust the properties to match the following settings:

- Set **Position** to (X: 0, Y: 15, Z: 0)
- Set **Rotation** to (X: 30°, Y: 0°, Z: 30°)
- Set **Scale** to 50%

Using these properties, you can adjust where and how the object appears within the scene.

Adjusting parametric properties

The cube you've added to the scene is a special object known as a parametric-shaped object. This means you can change the look of the object by adjusting its parameters.

Reality Composer offers quite a few parametric shapes that you can use to create weird and wonderful AR experiences.

For example:

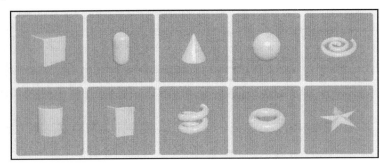

Feel free to experiment! :]

With the Properties panel still visible, expand the **Look** section to see what the cube shape has to offer.

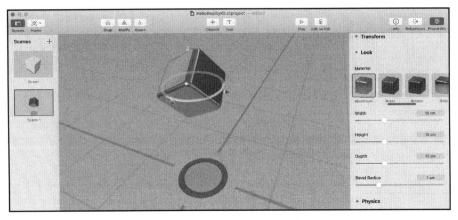

Here, you can change the material and shape of the cube. Adjust the cube, like so:

- Set the **Material** to **Aluminium**.
- Set the **Width** to 10cm.
- Set the **Height** to 10cm.
- Set the **Depth** to 10cm.
- Set the **Bevel Radius** to 1cm.

Your next step is to add some physics to your scene to bring it to life with some quick and dirty animation.

Enabling physics

Reality Composer comes with an easy-to-use but powerful built-in physics simulator. Adding basic animation to your virtual objects elevates the believability of any AR scene.

With the cube still selected, expand the **Physics** section on the Properties panel.

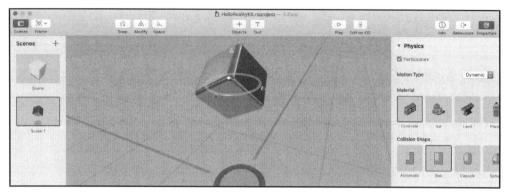

Check the **Participates** option to enable physics for the selected object. When the scene plays, the object will come to life and fall to the ground, just like a real object in the real world would due to gravity.

Motion Type

There are two options for Motion Type, which determines how the object will participate in the physics simulation:

- **Static**: When set to Static, the object will participate in the physics simulation, but the physics engine won't dynamically move it. You can animate the object by other means, and it will collide with other physics-enabled objects – like a baseball bat, for example.

- **Dynamic**: When set to Dynamic, the object will participate in the physics simulation, and the physics engine will dynamically move it. This could be a baseball, for example.

Select **Dynamic** to make the object participate dynamically in the physics simulation.

Physics Material

Your next step is to set up the **Physics Material** of the object. Reality Composer provides a few pre-configured material types.

These options control the object mass, material density, surface drag coefficient and restitution, or bounciness, of the object. So setting the material to concrete would make the object heavier and less bouncy than setting it to rubber, for example.

For this example, set the **Material** to **Concrete**.

Physics Collision Shape

Up next is setting the object's **Physics Collision Shape**, which defines a rough shape for the object using the least amount of geometry possible. This reduces the overhead the physics engine has to deal with when computing collisions between multiple objects.

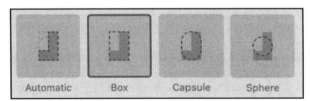

Reality Composer offers four basic shapes:

- **Automatic**: When you choose Automatic, Reality Composer automatically generates a low-polygon collision mesh based on the actual 3D model mesh. This should be your last resort if none of the other basic shapes work for you. This is the least performant collision shape.

- **Box**: Sets the collision mesh to a box shape. Useful for boxes, walls and flat objects, for example.

- **Capsule**: Setting the collision shape to capsule is useful for character bodies, for example.

- **Sphere**: Spheres are useful for round objects like balls. This is also the most performant collision shape.

Set the **Collision Shape** to **Box**.

Your basic AR scene is done now. Yay! Now wouldn't it be great if there was a way to test it? Well, actually, there is… and you'll do that next.

Playing scenes

Reality Composer has the ability to play the AR scene so that you can test it to find and debug any possible issues.

Click the **Play** button in the toolbar — but keep a watchful eye, because what you're about to see happens quickly.

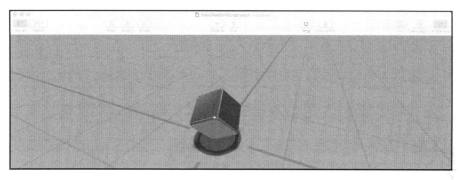

Did you see it? The cube comes alive, falls to the floor and bounces. Excellent!

Now wouldn't it be nice to experience the scene in augmented reality? That brings us to Reality files.

What are Reality files?

Reality Files contain an AR experience created with Reality Composer. They're archives that contain all of the required graphics, animations, textures and sounds that the AR scene requires. You can share the file and play it back on any app that supports AR Quick Look.

Exporting and sharing Reality files

To share your AR experience, you first have to export it.

Make sure you still have **Scene 1** selected and select **File ▸ Export ▸ Export Current Scene…** to export the scene as a **Reality** file.

Name the file **HelloRealityComposer.reality**, then click **Export**.

That's it; you're done. You've successfully created your first AR experience with Reality Composer.

To test it out on your device, find the file in Finder, then right-click it and select **Share ▸ AirDrop**. Finally, select your device from the list.

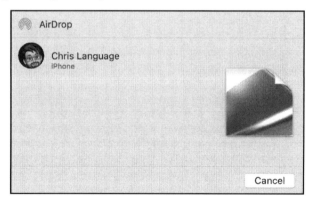

On your device, accept and save the file using **Files**, then open it.

A shiny metal cube magically drops on your desk. How cool is that?

> **Note**: You can find the final project and the exported Reality file inside the **final** folder.

Key points

Congratulations! You've reached the end of this chapter. Consider yourself now one full toe deep into the fantastic world of augmented reality. :]

Here are some of the key points covered in this chapter:

- **Reality Composer**: You now have a basic understanding of what Reality Composer is and what you can do with it.
- **Features and Limitations**: You have a good understanding of the feature set Reality Composer has to offer, along with its limitations.
- **Projects**: You know how to create your own Reality Composer projects.
- **UI**: You know your way around the user interface.
- **Creating Multiple Scenes**: It's super easy to give your project multiple scenes.
- **Content Library**: It's also easy to add virtual content to the scenes, especially with the wide range of objects to choose from the built-in content library.
- **Parametric Shapes**: You learned about parametric shapes and how to manipulate the parameters under the Properties panel.
- **Physics**: You got a quick introduction to basic physics and how easy it is to set up in Reality Composer.
- **Play and Debug**: You learned how to playtest your AR scenes with the Play option.
- **Export and Share**: Finally, you saw that once you've finished creating your experience, exporting it and sharing it is a breeze!

That's it for now. See you in the next chapter, where you'll learn about USDZ files and how they operate.

Chapter 4: USDZ Files & USD Python Tools

In the previous chapters, you explored the power of AR Quick Look. You also learned how to create your own AR experiences with Reality Composer using models from the built-in content library. But what about creating AR experiences with your own custom content?

The key technology behind AR Quick Look and Reality Composer is a file format known as **USDZ**.

In this chapter, you'll learn about USD and the USDZ file format. You'll also learn how to convert your own virtual content into this universal format using Python-based command-line tools. This knowledge will empower you to create your own USDZ content for both AR Quick Look and Reality Composer.

What is USD?

Before getting to USDZ, you need to understand the technology behind it: **Universal Scene Description (USD)**. This is a universal format to exchange 3D content. Pixar developed it to improve the graphics and animation workflow pipeline of large-scale animation productions.

USD has been under development since 2016. It's one of the core technologies behind stunning animation blockbusters like "Finding Dory" and "Cars".

Since Pixar open-sourced the technology, it's become an industry standard. Many of the big players within the 3D graphics and animation industry now back it.

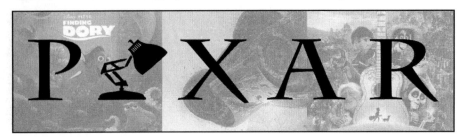

USD features

USD comes with an onslaught of great features. Here's a shortened list of just some of its key features:

- Robust schemas for the interchange of geometry, shading and skeletal deformation.
- High-performance data retrieval, object rendering and instancing.
- Ability to natively package user-selectable content variations.
- Future-friendly, flexible architecture designed to easily adapt to changing requirements.
- Powerful composition engine built with a focus on speed, scalability and collaboration.
- Supports Live Composition, Scalable to Complex scenes and Scene Graph.

USD is essentially a universal 3D file format. It's a C++ library that can read and write USD files with Python bindings.

There are three file extensions mainly associated with USD:

- **USDA**: Plain text file designed to be human-readable and easy to understand.
- **USDC**: Binary version of the USDA file, designed to be as efficient as possible.
- **USD**: Can be either a text file or a binary file.

> **Note**: You can easily convert USDA into USDC and vice-versa.

What is USDZ?

At WWDC 2018, Apple introduced AR Quick Look along with the new USDZ file format. As you know by now, **USD** stands for **Universal Scene Description**; the added **Z** merely indicates that it's a **ZIP** archive.

USDZ features

A number of critical features make USDZ an excellent choice for 3D content delivery:

- USDZ is essentially a distribution format for USD.

- USDZ contains all of the related files for a specific USD scene, packaged nicely in a single ZIP archive.

- USDZ is optimized specifically for sharing. It forms the basis behind AR Quick Look, which is supported on iOS, macOS and tvOS.

- USDZ supports Scalable to Complex scenes and Scene Graph.

- USDZ is an uncompressed archive that has 64-byte boundary-aligned files. This is the most efficient format for high-performance memory mapping.

A USDZ archive contains two types of files:

- **Scene Description Files**: These can be USD, USDA, USDC or even USDZ files.

- **Texture Files**: These can be PNG or JPEG image files.

USDZ tools

At WWDC 2019, Apple announced a new set of tools to help developers create their own USDZ files. These tools are known as **USDZ Tools** or the **USD Python Tools**.

USDZ Tools is a pre-compiled Python library containing binaries of Pixar's USD library for macOS. The tools allow you to convert, validate, generate and inspect USDZ files.

In the next section, you'll learn how to convert a 3D model into the USDZ file format.

Installing USDZ tools

Your first step is to download the USDZ Tools: https://apple.co/36TN9WJ

> **Note:** To download these tools, you need to log into the Apple Developer site using your Apple Developer login credentials.

When you open the above link, you'll see the following download page:

Expand the latest available version, then select the download link on the right:

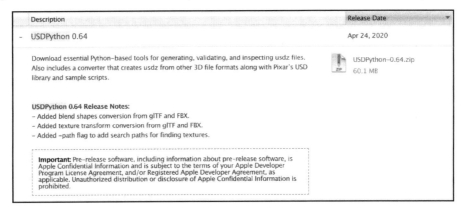

> **Note**: At the time of writing, the latest available version is **USDPython 0.64**, released on April 24th, 2020.

Once the ZIP file downloads, extract it. After it's extracted you should see the **USDPython-0.64.pkg** installer. Double-click the installer and follow the installation instructions to get the tools installed.

Once done, find and open **Applications/usdpython** in Finder. You'll see the following contents.

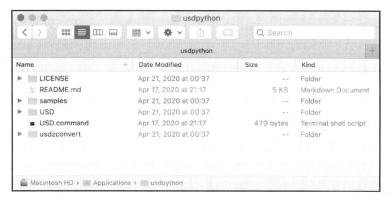

Here's what this is all about:

- **LICENSE**: The legal information about the tools.

- **README.md**: A detailed description of all the files contained in the archive. It's a good idea to read it.

- **samples**: A set of sample Python scripts that demonstrate how to use the USD Python library.

- **USD**: The precompiled Python library plus a suite of command-line tools from Pixar. You can use these tools to validate, check and inspect your USDZ files.

- **USD.command**: A command file that will set up the required environment variables for you.

- **usdconvert**: Contains the USDZ Converter tool and another special tool for fixing opacity issues.

Right-click the **USD.command** file and select **Open**. If you see the following security message, click **Open**.

A Terminal window opens with a prompt like:

```
Last login: Fri May  8 12:31:46 on ttys000
/Applications/usdpython/USD.command ; exit;
~ $ /Applications/usdpython/USD.command ; exit;
For FBX support, edit PYTHONPATH in this file (USD.command) or your shell configuration file
~ $
```

That's it, you're ready to go!

Reviewing the project

For this example, you'll use a cool AR drum set Reality Composer project. Open **starter/ARDrumSet.rcproject** in Reality Composer, then press the **Play** button to test it.

Click on any of the objects to hear how they sound. Nice!

Hey, wait a minute! There's a crucial piece missing: The kick drum is missing, which brings you to your next section.

Exporting 3D models

The first thing to do is to export the kick drum from the original 3D composition in a format that USDZ Tools supports.

> **Note**: For this example, you'll use Blender 2.8x to demonstrate a few important steps required to export your 3D models. You can apply this knowledge to any of the other modern 3D authoring tools. If you don't have Blender installed, feel free to skip this section.

Start Blender 2.8x and load the 3D model located at **starter/ARDrumSet.blend**.

Select the kick drum by **left-clicking** it. Press the **Backslash** key to isolate the drum from the rest of the composition.

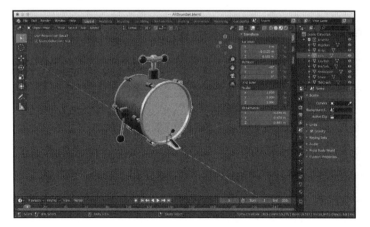

Look at the object transform information. Note that the drum has both a rotation and a scale applied to it.

It's a good idea to export your 3D objects with a zero rotation and scale of 1 transform because they are generally easier to work with at this size and with no rotation.

To fix this, make sure you've selected the drum, apply the current rotation and scale by pressing **Control-A**, then select **Apply ▸ Rotation & Scale**.

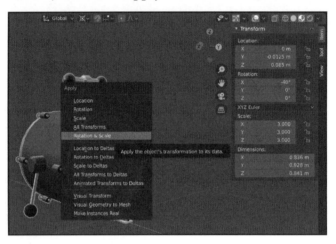

You've set the rotation to 0 and the scale to 1.

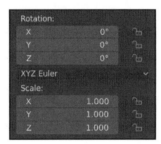

Perfect! You now need to fix the origin point of the object. You'll use the 3D Cursor to set it, so first make sure you've positioned the 3D Cursor at the **World Origin** point.

Press **Shift-S** to bring up the **Snap** pie menu, then select **Snap ▸ Cursor to World Origin**.

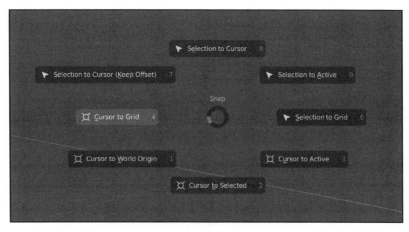

Done! Press **3** to switch into side orthographic view.

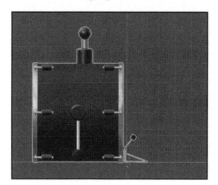

Press **G** to grab the object, then hold **Control** while moving the drum to the right until it centers with the World Origin.

Nicely done! **Right-click** the object to display the **Object Context Menu**. Select **Set Origin ▸ Origin to 3D Cursor** to move the object origin to the same location as the 3D Cursor.

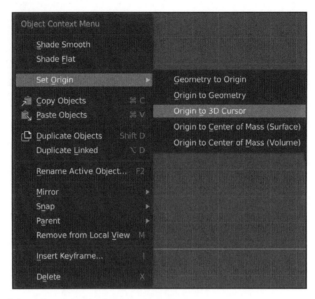

Excellent, your object is now ready to export!

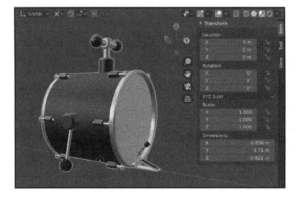

With the drum still selected, go to **File ▸ Export ▸ glTF 2.0 (.glb/.gltf)** to bring up the export options.

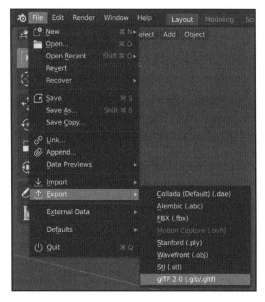

The following export options will appear:

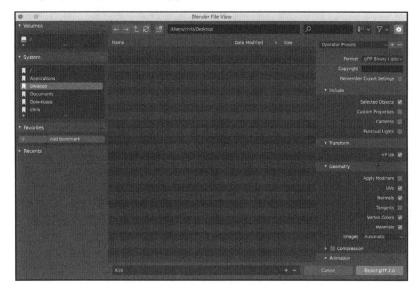

Set the export location to **Desktop**. Then go through the export options and check the following settings:

- **Include ▸ Selected Objects**. Now, only the selected model will export.
- **Transform ▸ +Y Up**. Converts Blender **+Z Up** to **+Y Up**, which is what Reality Composer uses.
- **Geometry ▸ Apply Modifiers**. Applies all necessary modifiers to the object geometry.
- **Geometry ▸ UVs**. Includes UV mapping information.
- **Geometry ▸ Normals**. Includes Normal information.
- **Geometry ▸ Vertex Colors**. Includes Vertex color information.
- **Geometry ▸ Materials**. Includes Material information.

Set the file name to **Kick**, then select **Export glTF 2.0** to finalize the export.

You've just exported the kick drum. You now have a file named **Kick.glb** on your **Desktop**. You can preview the file in Finder.

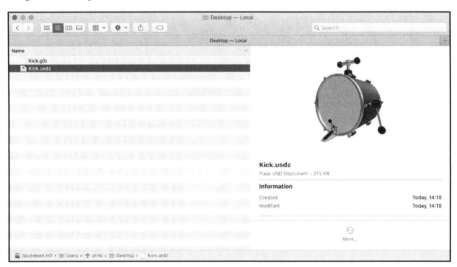

Fantastic!

> **Note**: Find the resulting exported file under **starter/Kick.glb**. For the sake of simplicity, this book assumes you've copied the **Kick.glb** file to your **Desktop**. Please make sure to adjust the paths accordingly if you're using a different path.

Converting 3D models to USDZ

It's time to convert **Kick.glb** into a USDZ file. To do this, jump back to the open **Terminal** window from the first section and execute the following command-line instructions:

```
cd /
cd Users/<YourUserName>/Desktop
```

This sets your active working directory to the same location as the **Kick.glb** file on your **Desktop**. Now, you don't have to worry about dealing with paths when providing parameters. You'll simply work out of the currently-active directory.

Using usdzconvert

For your next step, you'll use the **usdzconvert** tool. To find out more about the available options, execute the following command-line instructions to request detailed help information:

```
usdzconvert -h
```

```
~ $ usdzconvert -h
usdzconvert 0.62
usage: usdzconvert inputFile [outputFile]
                   [-h] [-f file] [-v]
                   [-url url]
                   [-copyright copyright]
                   [-copytextures]
                   [-metersPerUnit value]
                   [-loop]
                   [-no-loop]
                   [-iOS12]
                   [-m materialName]        [-texCoordSet name]
                   [-diffuseColor           r,g,b]
                   [-diffuseColor           <file> fr,fg,fb]
                   [-normal                 x,y,z]
                   [-normal                 <file> fx,fy,fz
                   [-emissiveColor          r,g,b]
                   [-emissiveColor          <file> fr,fb,fg]
                   [-metallic               c]
                   [-metallic               ch <file> fc]
                   [-roughness              c]
                   [-roughness              ch <file> fc]
                   [-occlusion              c]
                   [-occlusion              ch <file> fc]
                   [-opacity                c]
                   [-opacity                ch <file> fc]
                   [-clearcoat              c]
                   [-clearcoat              ch <file> fc]
                   [-clearcoatRoughness     c]
                   [-clearcoatRoughness     ch <file> fc]

Converts 3D model file to usd/usda/usdc/usdz.
```

This gives you a detailed list of options you can provide as input for usdzconvert.

Execute the following command-line instructions:

```
usdzconvert Kick.glb -v Kick.usdz
```

This tells the converter that you're providing **Kick.glb** as input and to produce **Kick.usdz** as output. -v instructs the converter to show verbose output.

The resulting output looks like this:

```
~ $ usdzconvert Kick.glb Kick.usdz -v
Input file: Kick.glb
  Mesh: Kick

Output file: Kick.usdz

usdARKitChecker: [Pass] Kick.usdz
```

The converter tool receives an input file named **Kick.glb** containing a single mesh called Kick. It then produces an output file named **Kick.usdz**. It finally checks the output file for any issues with **usdARKitChecker**. It found no issues, so the output file passed with flying colors.

That's it, you're done! You just created your first USDZ file.

Converting USDZ to USDA

To see what's inside the USDZ file, you need to convert it to a USDA file, which is the plain text representation of the USDZ.

Using usdcat

To do this, you'll use **usdcat**. This tool converts USDZ into USDA files.

To find out more about it, execute the following command-line instruction to request detailed help information:

```
usdcat -h
```

```
~ $ usdcat -h
usage: usdcat [-h] [-o file] [--usdFormat usda|usdb|usdc] [-l] [-f]
              [--flattenLayerStack] [--skipSourceFileComment]
              [--mask PRIMPATH[,PRIMPATH...]]
              inputFiles [inputFiles ...]

Write usd file(s) either as text to stdout or to a specified output file.
```

This gives you a detailed list of options that you can provide as input for the usdcat tool.

Execute the following command-line instructions:

```
usdcat Kick.usdz -o Kick.usda
```

The first parameter specifies the input file name as **Kick.usdz**. The -o specifies the output file as **Kick.usda**.

That's it, you've converted **Kick.usdz** to **Kick.usda**. You can now open the USDZ file with a normal text editor to see what the code looks like.

Inspecting and validating USDZ

Now that you've converted your 3D model into USDZ, you can inspect and validate the USDZ file.

Using usdtree

To get a high-level overview of the model hierarchy, you'll use the **usdtree** tool.

To find out more about this tool, execute the following command-line instruction to request detailed help information:

```
usdtree -h
```

```
~ $ usdtree -h
usage: usdtree [-h] [--unloaded] [--attributes] [--metadata] [--simple]
               [--flatten] [--flattenLayerStack]
               [--mask PRIMPATH[,PRIMPATH...]]
               inputPath

Writes the tree structure of a USD file. The default is to inspect a single
USD file. Use the --flatten argument to see the flattened (or composed) Stage
tree. Special metadata "kind" and "active" are always shown if authored unless
--simple is provided.
```

This gives you a detailed list of options that you can provide as input for the usdtree tool.

Execute the following command-line instructions:

```
usdtree Kick.usdz
```

The **Kick.usdz** parameter specifies the input file name.

The resulting output looks like this:

```
~ $ usdtree Kick.usdz
/
`--Kick [def Xform] (kind = component)
    |--Materials [def Scope]
    |   |--Rubber [def Material]
    |   |   `--surfaceShader [def Shader]
    |   |--Plastic [def Material]
    |   |   `--surfaceShader [def Shader]
    |   |--Silver [def Material]
    |   |   `--surfaceShader [def Shader]
    |   |--Red [def Material]
    |   |   `--surfaceShader [def Shader]
    |   `--White [def Material]
    |       `--surfaceShader [def Shader]
    `--Geom [def Scope]
        `--Kick [def Xform]
            |--primitive_0 [def Mesh]
            |--primitive_1 [def Mesh]
            |--primitive_2 [def Mesh]
            |--primitive_3 [def Mesh]
            `--primitive_4 [def Mesh]
```

This is a quick way to get an overview of your model hierarchy.

Using usdchecker

Finally, to validate the generated USDZ and to make sure the file is compliant, you'll use the **usdchecker** tool.

To find out more about this tool, execute the following command-line instructions to request detailed help information:

```
usdchecker -h
```

```
~ $ usdchecker -h
usage: usdchecker [-h] [-s] [-p] [-o [OUTFILE]] [--arkit] [-d] [-v]
                  [inputFile]
Utility for checking the compliance of a given USD stage or a USDZ package.
```

This gives you a detailed list of options that you can provide as input for the usdchecker tool.

Execute the following command-line instructions:

```
usdchecker Kick.usdz -v
```

The **Kick.usdz** parameter specifies the input file name. Finally, the –v parameter specifies verbose output.

The resulting output looks like this:

```
~ $ usdchecker Kick.usdz -v
Checking package <Kick.usdz>.
Success!
```

The file is validated and checked. Excellent, your USDZ file passed the check with flying colors!

Importing USDZ assets

Now that your USDZ file is ready to go, open **starter/ARDrumSet.rcproject** again with Reality Composer.

Yes, you've already established that the kick drum is missing. You're about to fix that! :]

To import a new USDZ asset, select the **Objects (+)** button to access the built-in asset library. Then select the **Import** button at the top-right to add custom assets.

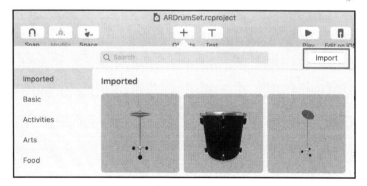

Find and select **Kick.usdz** on your **Desktop**, then select **Import** to complete the process.

This imports the kick drum into the active scene, but to the right of the other drums. To position it properly, make sure you still have the kick drum selected, then open the **Properties** panel. Set the **Position** to (X: 0cm, Y: 0,24cm, Z: 0cm) and set the Rotations to (X: -180°, Y: 0, Z: 180°).

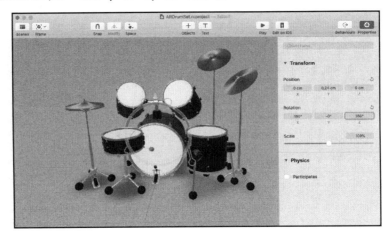

The kick drum is now present within the scene.

Your next step is to make it play like all the other drums. Select **Behaviors** at the top-right to open the Behaviors panel.

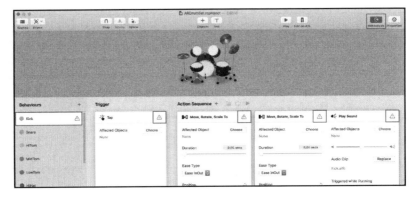

This is where you add interactions, animations and sound effects to all the virtual content in the scene.

Hang on, did you notice all those **Alert** signs?

The alerts tell you that there's something wrong with the behavior. In this case, it's because you haven't connected the behavior to the kick drum yet.

To connect the **Trigger Tap** event, select **Choose**, then select the **kick drum**. The Choose button will change into a **Done** button. Select it to complete the connection.

Now that you've connected the event to the kick drum, the alert indicator disappears. Follow the same process for all the other alerts to connect them all to the kick drum.

There's one final step: You need to reset all of the **Position Actions** so they don't move the kick drum when the user taps it. Select the Reset Position button – the curly back arrow – to clear any positional information.

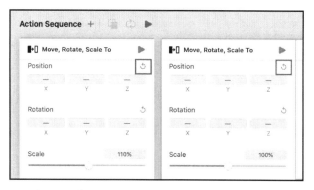

Now, when the user triggers the action sequence, it won't affect the kick drum's position.

Excellent, you're all done! You can now **Play** the scene to test your awesome AR Drum Set. Feel free to export the scene as a Reality file, then send it to your iPhone to test it in augmented reality.

Key points

Well done, you've just reached the end of this chapter.

In this chapter, you learned:

- All about USD and USDZ.
- That it's easy to get started with the new USDZ Tools, also known as the USD Python Tools, created by Pixar.
- How to prepare your 3D content for export by setting the model's origin point, rotation and scale.
- All about converting 3D content into the USDZ format with the usdzconvert tool.
- How to convert USDZ into USDA with the usdcat tool.
- How to inspect USDZ files with usdtree and test them with usdchecker.

Where to go from here?

Here are a few recommended links you can explore to advance your knowledge on this topic:

- **WWDC 2018 & 2019 Videos about USD**: https://apple.co/2YmYX3B
- **Pixar – Introduction to USD**: https://bit.ly/2CeiYPK
- **Pixar – USDZ File Format Specification**: https://bit.ly/2wDDK5j

It's super-easy to convert your own content into USDZ. The only thing left to do is to go forth and augment your world with your very own content!

Chapter 5: Reality Converter & PBR Materials

In the previous chapter, you learned how to convert virtual content into a usable USDZ file format with USD Python Tools. However, the conversion process is tedious and not user-friendly.

In early 2020, Apple introduced a new app specifically designed to make USDZ conversion as simple and user-friendly as possible: **Reality Converter**.

Reality Converter

What is Reality Converter?

Reality Converter is a macOS-based app that makes it easy to convert, view and customize USDZ content. It offers a simple drag and drop interface with support for common 3D file formats like .obj, .gltf and .usd.

It allows you to customize material properties with your own textures and edit the USDZ metadata. With its WYSIWYG (What You See Is What You Get) design, you can easily preview your virtual content under various lighting conditions. Once you're happy with the end result, it's simple to export your model as a USDZ file.

> **Note**: At the time of writing, Reality Converter is still in Beta and access to it requires an Apple Developer account. Future versions might install along with Xcode, just as Reality Composer does.

Adding a 3D model

Download **Reality Converter** from this link: https://apple.co/38LbwqM. Then install and start it.

The interface is quite simple, with a toolbar at the top and a preview of your 3D content below. If you haven't loaded any content yet, you'll see a prompt to drag and drop 3D content onto the app.

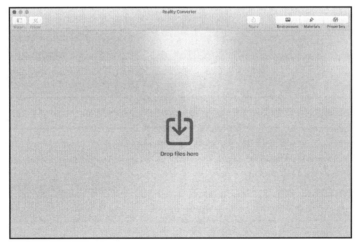

There's a low-poly ball model for you to use in **starter/Models/Ball.glb**.

Bring the model into your project by going to **Finder**, then dragging and dropping **Ball.glb** on the app where it says **Drop files here**.

Reality Converter instantly recognizes the .glb file and imports the low-poly ball, a basic gray sphere, into the scene.

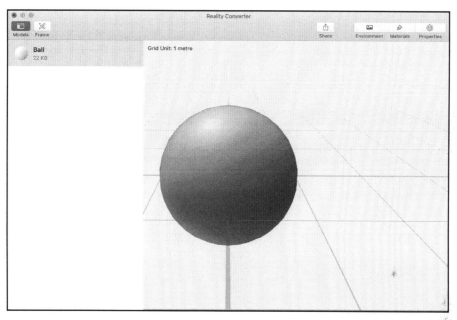

At the top-left of the toolbar, select the **Models** button to see which models you can use. Currently, only a **Ball** is available. For simplicity's sake, you'll work with this one model.

The ball isn't very impressive at this point, but with the magic of **Physically Based Rendering (PBR)** materials, you'll turn this gray sphere into a glorious-looking soccer ball.

PBR materials

Reality Composer and the USDZ file format use the PBR lighting model, which offers diffuse lighting with a realistic abstraction of physical lights and materials.

The material defines the basic lighting model along with various other properties like its color, specularity, reflectivity, shininess, roughness and even its opacity.

Materials define properties of the material itself by using a solid color or a texture.

Textures are flat, 2D images that wrap around the 3D model geometry using special texture coordinates, known as UV-coordinates.

The sphere in your project has already been UV-mapped. You just need to apply some textures to it.

In the top toolbar, select the **Materials** panel. The ball has no materials assigned to it, so Reality Converter has created a **defaultConverterMaterial** for you.

If your 3D model had more than one material assigned to it, you'd be able to select it here.

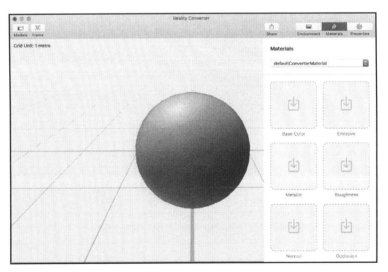

Now, you're ready to add texture to the ball.

> **Note**: Follow each of the following steps to add textures to the model. This will let you see the impact each individual texture has on the final model in detail.

Base Color map

The **Base Color**, or **Diffuse**, map gives the geometry a **base color** texture. Typically, this texture defines what the object is regardless of any lights and special effects.

In **Finder** inside **starter/Materials**, find **ball_Diffuse.png**. Drag and drop it into the **Base Color** channel.

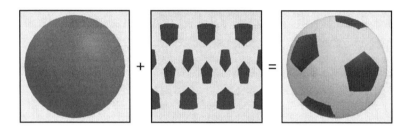

The full-color map noticeably defines the gray sphere as a basic ball. Also, note that the rest of the ball's surface is flat and not very shiny.

Normal map

The **Normal** map is a special kind of map that controls how light reflects off the surface. Technically, it defines how the surface combines with detailed surface normal data that bends reflected light off the surface. It ultimately makes the surface appear to have more detail in its geometry without needing a higher poly count.

Now, find **ball_Normal.png** in **Finder** inside **starter/Textures**. Drag and drop it into the **Normal** channel.

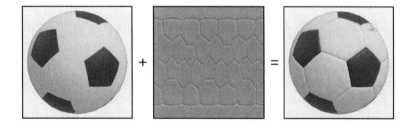

The ball no longer has a flat surface. You can now make a clear distinction between the black pentagon patches and the white hexagon patches. It also appears as if the geometry of the ball increased, which isn't the case. That's just the beauty of a Normal map at work.

Occlusion map

The **Occlusion**, or **Ambient Occlusion**, map defines the amount of ambient light that reaches certain parts of the geometry. When looking at real-world objects, you'll notice that light typically struggles to reach tight spaces, like the lines of stitching between the ball's patches.

In **Finder** inside **starter/Textures**, find **ball_Occlusion.png**. Drag and drop it into the **Occlusion** channel.

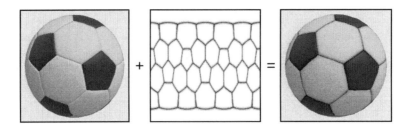

Use the grayscale image to darken the creases between the patches of the ball, making it look like they're blocking out the ambient light. This makes the ball look much more realistic.

Metallic map

One of the key trademarks of PBR materials is the use of **Metallic** maps that define how metallic or dielectric — that is, non-metallic or plastic — a surface is.

In **Finder** inside **starter/Textures**, find **ball_Metallic.png**. Drag and drop it into the **Metallic** channel.

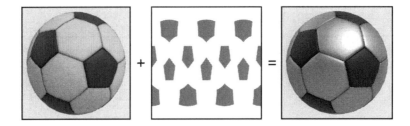

The grayscale image defines the fully-metallic parts as white, the fully-dielectric parts as black and everything else as in between. The white patches on the ball instantly turn metallic and the black patches turn somewhat dielectric.

Roughness map

PBR materials use **Roughness** maps to define how smooth or rough a surface is. They approximate the microscopic detail of real-world surfaces to produce a shiny or matte appearance.

In **Finder** inside **starter/Textures**, find **ball_Roughness.png**, then drag and drop it into the **Roughness** channel.

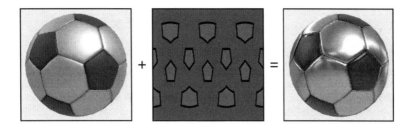

The grayscale image defines the fully-matte parts as white, the fully-smooth parts as black and everything else as in between. The previously-white patches turned into somewhat reflective silver patches and the black patches turned matte with a super shiny edge.

Emissive map

The **Emissive** map overrides all lighting and shading information to create a light-emitting effect.

In **Finder** inside **starter/Textures**, find **ball_Emissive.png**, then drag and drop it into the **Emissive** channel.

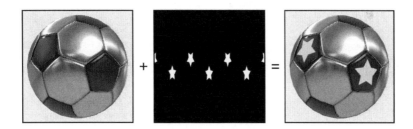

The full-color image defines white areas of the surface that will ignore all light and shadow information. The black areas define the non-lit areas of the surface.

Clearcoat map

The **Clearcoat** map simulates a thin reflective layer on top of a surface, like the transparent coating of a car's paint job. It can also represent varnish, water or anything else that benefits from multiple layers.

In **Finder** inside **starter/Textures**, find **ball_Clearcoat.png**. Drag and drop it into the **Clearcoat** channel.

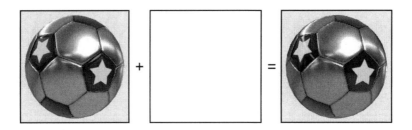

The grayscale image controls the clearcoat's intensity. In this case, you give the entire ball a glossy coat.

Clearcoat Roughness map

The **Clearcoat Roughness** map works in conjunction with the Clearcoat map, defining how smooth or rough the clearcoat on top of the surface is.

In **Finder** inside **starter/Textures**, find **ball_ClearcoatRoughness.png**. Drag and drop it into the **Clearcoat Roughness** channel.

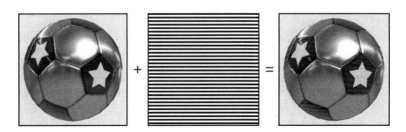

The grayscale image defines the rough-coated parts as white and the smooth-coated parts as black. In this case, the ball alternates between rough-coated stripes and smooth-coated stripes.

Opacity map

The **Opacity** map makes certain parts of the geometric surface appear either opaque or transparent.

In **Finder** inside **starter/Textures**, find **ball_Opacity.png**, then drag and drop it into the **Opacity** channel.

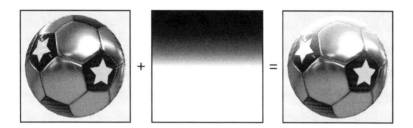

The grayscale image defines the completely-opaque parts as white and the completely-transparent parts as black. In this case, the top half of the ball fades from completely opaque to completely transparent.

Environment

Reality Converter has another cool feature that allows you to preview your virtual content under various lighting conditions.

To try it, select the **Environment** panel in the toolbar at the top. Enable the **Show Environment** checkbox.

Reality Converter comes with a great selection of environments from which to choose. They simulate various lighting conditions so you can test your virtual content in different environments.

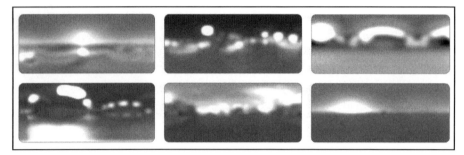

Test a few now. Here's what the ball looks like with each of the available environment maps:

The environment has a drastic effect on the look and feel of the ball. Overall, the ball performs well under all of the above lighting conditions. Great!

Exposure

Exposure controls the amount of light to which the virtual content is exposed. Reality Converter allows you to test that, too.

With the **Environment** panel still open, grab the **Exposure** dial and drag it to the left, then slowly drag it to the right.

This will simulate going from an extremely dark exposure to an extremely light exposure.

Again, the ball holds up under these extreme lighting conditions. This is a good way to test the emissive behavior of your virtual content. In this case, note how the star emblem doesn't fade from dark to bright. Excellent!

Properties

Your model is almost done, but there's one step left to do: You need to set the metadata for your virtual content before you share it with the world.

Select the **Properties** panel at the top of the toolbar.

Fill in the **Copyright** information. You can also set the **Base Unit** scale of your content.

Sharing

You've finished your model. It's time to test it on your iPhone or iPad.

Select the **Share** button at the top of the toolbar, then select **Airdrop**.

Select your phone, and you're done. It's that simple!

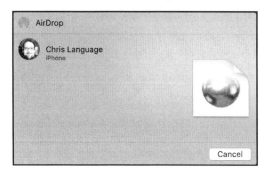

Exporting USDZ

Now that you've added all of the textures and tested your 3D model under various lighting and real-life conditions, it's time to export the USDZ file.

Select **File ▸ Export**, then provide a filename and destination for your USDZ file. Select **Save** to export the USDZ file.

Fantastic! You've just converted your first 3D model using Reality Converter.

> **Note**: Find the final exported version of the ball under **final/Ball.usdz**.

Key points

You've reached the end of the chapter and you now know how to convert your content using Reality Converter.

Glance back at what you've covered:

- **Reality Converter**: You now have a good idea of what Reality Converter is and what it can do.

- **PBR Materials**: As an added bonus, you've learned about Physically Based Rendering materials and how various types of texture construct a complex but realistic-looking PBR material.

- **Environment**: Testing your virtual content under various lighting conditions is a breeze.

- **Exposure**: Testing your virtual content with different lighting exposures is just as easy.

- **Sharing and Exporting**: There's a dedicated Share button if you want to quickly test your content on a device. Exporting the USDZ file is as simple as saving your project.

Section II: Reality Composer & Image Tracking

In this section, you'll dive a little deeper into augmented reality and learn about image anchors and tracking. You'll also create an interactive AR Business Card that you can show off to your friends, making them green with envy.

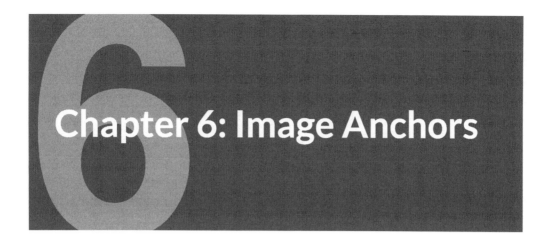

Chapter 6: Image Anchors

In this section, you'll dive a little deeper into augmented reality and learn about image anchors and tracking. You'll also create an interactive **AR Business Card** that you can show off to your friends, making them green with envy.

While this image might look real, only the card lying on the table exists in the physical world; the buttons, photo and contact information are all virtual. Boom, mind blown! :]

What are image anchors?

Image-based AR has been around for quite some time. Many modern, camera-equipped smart devices are capable of AR, usually by using **tracking cards** and a technique known as **marker-based augmented reality**, which is now known as *image anchors* in Reality Composer.

The image serves as an anchor point on a real-world surface. A special algorithm then analyzes the camera data to determine the image's position, scale and orientation. You then use that tracking information to project, scale and place virtual content overtop the camera's image.

A great example of this technology is *Om Nom: Candy Flick*, a surprisingly fun little augmented reality game. The goal of that game is to flick candy toward Om Nom and hope he catches it.

Unfortunately, you lose the tracking the moment the image goes outside of the camera's view, spoiling the entire AR experience.

Creating an image anchor-based experience in Reality Composer only takes a few steps, which you're about to do next.

Creating an image anchor project

The first step in the process is to create a project for your AR experience. Open **Reality Composer**, and it will open Finder to locate an existing project. You want to create a new project instead, so select **New Document**.

Reality Composer gives you the opportunity to choose the type of anchor you need for your AR experience. Select **Image** and make sure to uncheck **Use template content**. Complete the process by clicking **Choose**.

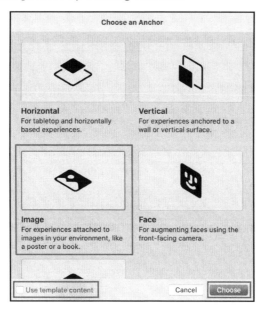

Reality Composer creates an empty image-based anchor project with a single scene. Because you disabled the option to use template content, no other content exists.

With the scene selected and the **Properties** panel open, rename the scene to **Main**.

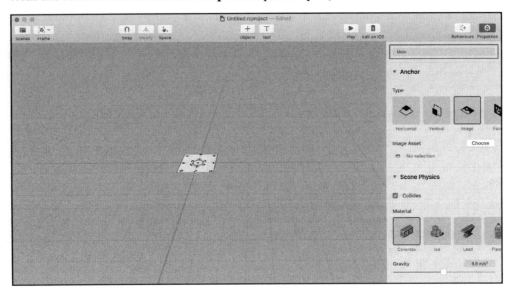

This is the main scene for the AR experience. Note that the **Anchor** type is set to **Image**. You can leave the rest of the settings at their default values.

There's one little issue, though: you've created the project, but you haven't saved it yet. To save your project, select **File ▸ Save** from the main menu.

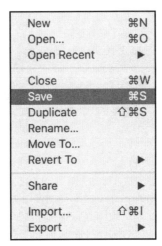

Change the project name to **ARBusinessCard.rcproject**, then set the destination to a location of your choice. For example, the **Desktop**.

Click **Save** to complete the process.

Excellent, you now have a new project saved to your local device. The next time you want to open your project, double-click **ARBusinessCard.rcproject** in **Finder**, and it will open in Reality Composer.

Adding an image anchor

The next step is to choose the image to use as the image anchor. For this project, you'll need some kind of image to track, so you'll use a specially-issued, one-of-a-kind Ray Wenderlich Team card.

The entire AR experience will spawn out of this card — that is, once you bring the card into view of the camera.

> **Note**: You're welcome to print a copy of the card for testing purposes. You can find the image at **starter/resources/RWTeamCard.png**. The physical size of the card is 9cm in length and 5cm in width.

When creating or choosing an image to use as an image anchor, there are three basic factors to consider:

- **Quality**: Make sure you're using a crisp, clear image. A blurry or dirty image might be difficult to recognize.
- **Scale**: Always think of the environment surrounding the image. A big, poster-sized image is recognizable from a greater distance than a small business card. If your AR experience requires more space, consider using images with a larger scale.
- **Uniqueness**: When creating AR experiences for a collection of images, make sure the images aren't similar enough that the recognition algorithm gets confused and mistakes one image for another. Consider using unique, noisy backgrounds, markers or patterns.

With the **Main** scene still selected and the Properties panel open, click the **Choose** button next to **Image Asset**.

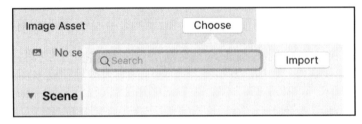

A pop-up with available images appears, but you'll notice that it shows no available images yet. That's because you still need to import the image that you'll use for the anchor.

Click the **Import** button, then locate the image **starter/resources/RWTeamCard.png**. Once selected, click **Import** to complete the process.

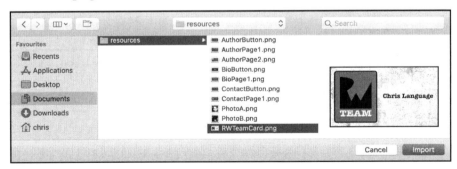

Reality Composer imports the selected image. During this step, Reality Composer analyzes the image to ensure it's suitable for recognition.

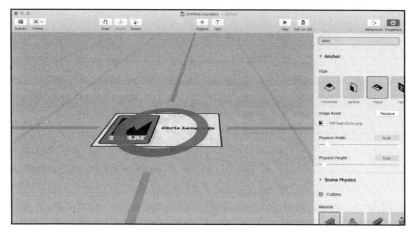

If you've selected a poor-quality image, Reality Composer gives you a warning, stating that the selected image is not suitable for recognition. No warning is usually a good sign that you've provided an adequate image for an anchor.

Now, you could adjust the physical width and height of your anchor image; however, in this case, it's not necessary because you've already scaled the image correctly to represent its physical counterpart.

You've set your image anchor, and it's visible within the main scene. You're ready for the next step.

Adding an image

Your business card is very basic at the moment. A good starting point to make it more exciting is to add your photo.

Reality Composer refers to images as **Frames**. You can choose between a bordered frame and a borderless frame. The great part about frames is that they support transparent images, allowing you to create stunning experiences.

Click the **Objects** button at the top menu bar to open the content library, and then search for **Frame**. You'll find two frames within the **Arts** section. Double-click the borderless frame to add it to the scene.

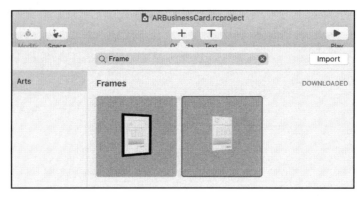

Next, rename the frame object to **PhotoA**. Then, set the **Position** to (X: 2cm, Y: 1.5cm, Z: 0cm) and the **Scale** to 30% in the **Transform** section.

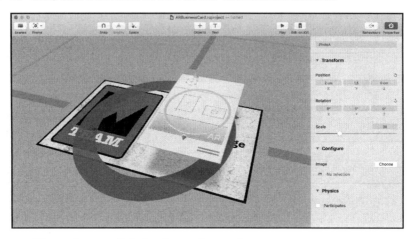

The frame will now hover slightly above the card.

In the **Configure** section, click **Choose** for the **Image**, then **Import** a new image.

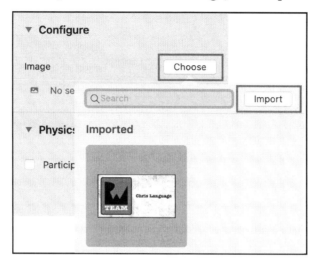

Instead of importing a single image, this time, you'll import all of the images that you'll use for this AR experience.

Inside **starter/resources**, select the first image, **AuthorButton.png**. While holding the **Shift** key, select the last image, **PhotoB.png**; this action will select all of the images from the first to the last. After they're all highlighted, click **Import** to complete the process.

Reality Composer selects the first imported image by default.

Within the **Configure** section, for the **Image**, click **Replace**, then choose **PhotoA.png** from the imported images.

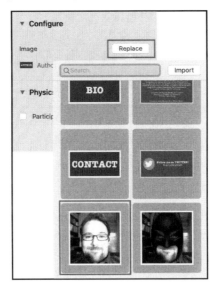

Excellent! You replaced the image with the ever-so-handsome **PhotoA.png**.

With the imaged added, you're ready for the next step.

Adding 3D text

To make things pop a bit more, your next step is to add some 3D text to the AR experience.

Add another **Object** to the scene, but this time do a search for **Text**. Double-click the **Text** object to add it to the scene.

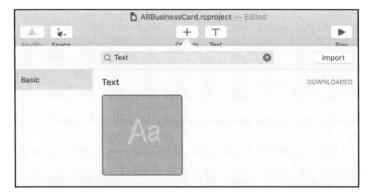

> **Note**: There's also a dedicated Text button next to the Object button if you prefer to use that.

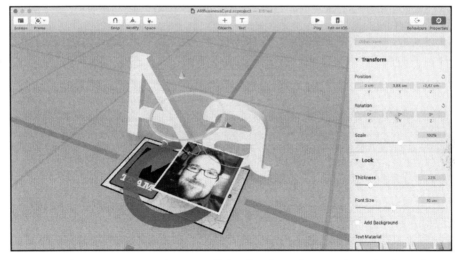

The new text object is way too big. You'll fix that by taking a closer look at the available properties.

In the Properties panel, rename the text object to **AuthorName**. Inside the **Transform** section, set the **Position** to (X: 2cm, Y: 1.7cm, Z: 1.7cm) and the **Rotation** to (X: -90°, Y: 0°, Z: 0°). Leave the **Scale** at 100%.

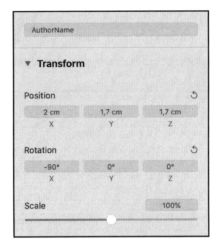

Within the **Look** section, set the **Thickness** to 20% and the **Font Size** to 0.5cm. Select **Glossy Paint** for **Text Material** and keep the **Text Color** as **White**.

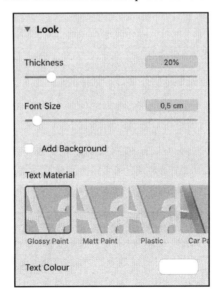

Within the **Text** section, change the text contents to **Chris Language**. Set the **Font** to **American Typewriter** and the **Style** to **Bold** aligned **Vertically** and **Horizontally**.

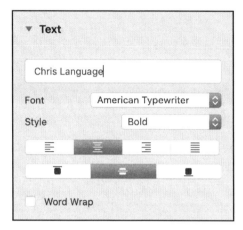

Once done, you'll see the following result:

Congratulations, you just added 3D text to your AR experience.

Completing the scene

You're actually creating the entire AR experience, even the buttons and the pop-ups, using only frames.

Now that you know how to add and configure images, add the rest using the following properties:

- **PhotoB** at **Position** (X: 2cm, Y: 1.5cm, Z: 0cm) and a **Scale** of 30%.

- **BioPage** at **Position** (X: 1.3cm, Y: 3.5cm, Z: -5cm) with a **Rotation** of (X: 45°, Y: 0°, Z: 0°) and a **Scale** of 78%.

- **AuthorPage1** at **Position** (X: 1.3cm, Y: 3.5cm, Z: -5cm) with a **Rotation** of (X: 45°, Y: 0°, Z: 0°) and a **Scale** of 78%.
- **AuthorPage2** at **Position** (X: 1.3cm, Y: 3.5cm, Z: -5cm) with a **Rotation** of (X: 45°, Y: 0°, Z: 0°) and a **Scale** of 78%.
- **ContactPage** at **Position** (X: 1.3cm, Y: 3.5cm, Z: -5cm) with a **Rotation** of (X: 45°, Y: 0°, Z: 0°) and a **Scale** of 78%.
- **BioButton** at **Position** (X: 6cm, Y: 1cm, Z: -1.6cm) and a **Scale** of 15%.
- **AuthorButton** at **Position** (X: 6cm, Y: 1cm, Z: 0cm) and a **Scale** of 15%.
- **ContactButton** at **Position** (X: 6cm, Y: 1cm, Z: 1.6cm) and a **Scale** of 15%.

Once you're done, the final result will look like this:

Editing on iOS

Reality Composer has a neat feature that allows you to stay productive while on the go. You can easily transfer a project to Reality Composer on your iPad or iPhone. No more excuses for you, you can now continue working even while commuting to and from work.

Start Reality Composer on your iPhone or iPad. Leave the app running and the device unlocked.

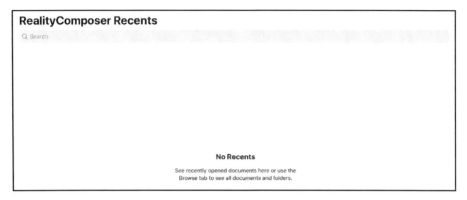

If this is the first time you do this, you won't see any recent available projects, but that'll change soon.

Back in **Reality Composer** on **macOS**, click **Edit on iOS** in the top menu bar.

You'll now see a list of all available devices with Reality Composer running.

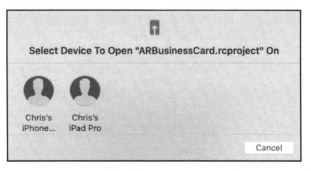

Select the device you want to transfer the project to, such as your iPad.

A connection request will appear on the device. Click **Accept** to allow the project to transfer to the device.

Wait for a second while the project synchronizes with the device.

Once done, Reality Composer on macOS will indicate that the project is currently on your device.

Now, you can continue editing the project on your iPad or iPhone.

Once you've made all of your changes, click **Done** in the top-left corner to transfer all of your changes back to Reality Composer on macOS.

> **Note**: While editing this particular project on your iPhone or iPad, you may have noticed some flickering on the images. This phenomenon is known **Z-Fighting**, and it happens because you've positioned the images on top of one another. This won't be a problem for this particular project, so ignore it for now.

Key points

You've reached the end of this chapter, well done. You've now added all of the required objects to the scene. You can grab a copy of the final project here: **final/ARBusinessCard/ARBusinessCard.rcproject**.

Here's a quick recap of what you learned:

- **Image Anchors**: You learned about image anchors, marker-based augmented reality that uses tracking cards or images.

- **Image Anchor Project**: You created an Image Anchor Project in Reality Composer and learned that linking and configuring a particular image to the anchor is also quite simple.

- **Image Anchor Considerations**: There are a few things to consider when creating or choosing an image to use as an image anchor. Quality, scale and uniqueness play a massive role.

- **Frame Objects**: You added and configured a few Frame objects, better known as images, to the scene.

- **3D Text Objects**: You also added and configured a 3D Text object to the scene.

- **Editing on iOS**: Need to continue working while on the go? No problem, you learned how to transfer the project to your iPhone to get the job done.

With all of the overlapping images, you probably guessed that the AR experience isn't quite done yet. In the next chapter, you'll bring all of the objects to life with clever animation and basic interaction.

Chapter 7: Behaviors, Triggers & Actions

This chapter continues where the previous one left off. The AR Business Card scene already contains all of the required objects, but the AR experience is rather dull.

To spice things up, you'll add animations and sound effects to the objects within the scene. You'll implement these features using behaviors, triggers and actions.

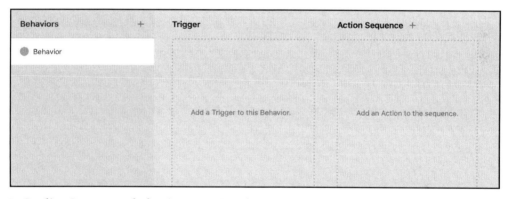

In Reality Composer, behaviors consist of a trigger component and an action sequence component. In this chapter, you'll use all of these components to build out your AR experience.

> **Note:** You can use your final project from the previous chapter or load **starter/ARBusinessCard/ARBusinessCard.rcproject** in Reality Composer. The rest of this chapter continues building from this point onwards.

What are behaviors?

Behaviors allow users to interact with objects within a Reality Composer scene without you, the developer, having to add code. Instead, you assign each behavior to a specific object.

Behaviors consist of two components: a **trigger**, which defines how and when a behavior activates, and an **action sequence**, which defines what happens to the object when the trigger event occurs.

Available behaviors

Reality Composer comes loaded with some behavior presets that cover the most common interactions for AR scenes. These behavior presets are also a good starting point when you want to build custom behaviors.

Here's the current list of behavior presets:

Here's what each behavior does:

- **Tap & Flip**: When the user **taps** a predefined object, that object bounces and flips over via a **jump and flip** action.

- **Tap & Play Sound**: When the user **taps** a predefined object, the object uses a **play a sound effect** action to emit a sound effect from its position.

- **Tap & Add Force**: When the user **taps** a predefined object with physics enabled, the object uses an **add force** action to move in a certain direction.

- **Start Hidden**: When the AR scene **starts**, a predefined object performs a **hide** action and becomes invisible.

- **Wait & Show**: When the AR scene **starts**, a predefined object performs a **wait** action and then a **show** action. This makes an object appear after a set period of time.

- **Proximity & Jiggle**: When the user comes within a certain **proximity** of a predefined object, the object performs a **jiggle** action.

- **Custom**: This behavior is empty, allowing you to define your own trigger and sequence of actions.

What are triggers?

Each behavior has a **trigger** component, which defines the event that activates the behavior.

You can assign a trigger to one or more objects within the scene. When the assigned object fulfills the event requirements, the behavior triggers and its action sequence component plays out.

Available triggers

Here's the current list of available triggers:

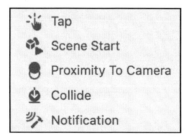

Here's what each trigger does:

- **Tap**: Triggers the behavior when the user **taps** the predefined object.

- **Scene Start**: Triggers the behavior when the AR scene **starts**.

- **Proximity To Camera**: Triggers the behavior when the predefined object is within a certain **proximity** of the camera.

- **Collide**: Triggers the behavior when predefined objects **collide**.
- **Notification**: Triggers the behavior when the predefined object receives a notification from Xcode.

What are actions?

Reality Composer is a codeless environment, so you don't need any prior coding knowledge to create interactive AR experiences. To overcome the need for code, Reality Composer introduces the concept of **actions**.

Actions let you make objects in the scene perform various functions. For example, moving from one position to another, playing sound effects and music, applying physics impulses and performing animations.

Actions are part of a behavior. Once the user triggers the behavior, the actions component plays out in a sequence or in parallel, depending on how you have things configured.

You can assign an action to one or more objects within the scene. When the action plays, it will only affect those objects.

Available actions

Here's the current list of available actions:

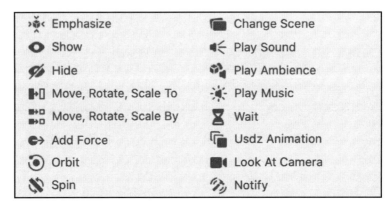

Here's what each actions does:

- **Emphasize**: Calls attention to the object with an animation.
- **Show**: Uses an animation to make an object visible.
- **Hide**: Makes an object invisible with an animation.
- **Move, Rotate, Scale To**: Transforms the object's position, rotation and scale *to* a specified transform.
- **Move, Rotate, Scale By**: Transforms an object's position, rotation and scale *by* a specified transform.
- **Add Force**: Applies an impulse force to an object.
- **Orbit**: Makes one object orbit another predefined object.
- **Spin**: Makes an object spin in place.
- **Change Scene**: Transitions from the current scene to another scene.
- **Play Sound**: Plays a sound that emits from a predefined object within the scene in the 3D environment.
- **Play Ambience**: Plays audio that emits from the scene's anchor point in the 3D environment.
- **Play Music**: Plays music or sound effects over the entire scene, disregarding any 3D positional information.
- **Wait**: Waits for a predefined time.
- **USDZ Animation**: Plays a specified animation on the object.
- **Look At Camera**: Tells an object to adjust its own rotation to face the camera's current position.
- **Notify**: Tells an object to send a notification to Xcode.

Adding a behavior preset

With the starter project open, you'll add a basic behavior preset to all of the objects within the scene. In this case, you'll hide the objects when the scene first starts and then have them reappear with some flair.

Open the Behaviors panel by selecting it in the top bar.

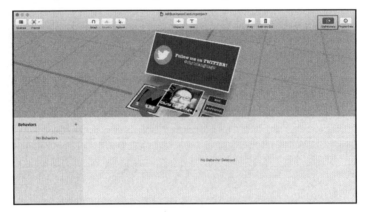

The Behaviors panel will now appear at the bottom of the scene view.

Select all of the objects within the scene by pressing **Command-A**. By selecting all of the objects, you can assign a single behavior preset to your selection, which saves a lot of time.

Click the + button next to Behaviors to add a behavior preset, and select **Start Hidden**.

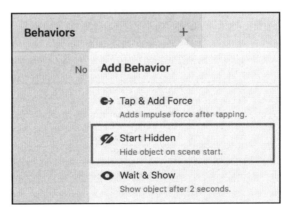

Reality Composer creates a new behavior from the selected preset and assigns it to all of the selected objects within the scene.

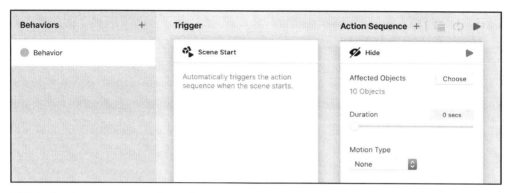

This behavior preset consists of two components: a **Scene Start** trigger, which will activate the behavior when the AR scene starts, and an action sequence that contains a **Hide** action assigned to 10 objects. Starting the scene will trigger the action sequence, which will hide all of the objects within the scene.

Reality Composer names newly-created behaviors **Behavior** by default; however, it's good practice to give your behaviors a more descriptive name.

Rename the behavior you just created to **Start**.

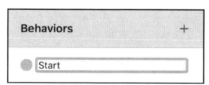

This behavior is the starting point for your entire scene.

Next, test the action sequence by playing it. Click the **Play** button next to the **Action Sequence** label to see what happens.

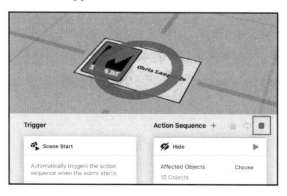

Notice the **Play** button turns into a **Stop** button, and all of the objects in the scene disappear as the action sequence plays.

> **Note**: Each defined action has its own Play button. This allows you to trigger only that individual action to see what it does on its own.

Adding action sequences

Now that you've hidden the scene objects on start, you'll use more action sequences to show these objects later.

Adding a Show action

The **Show** action lets you make an invisible object visible with a basic animation. Your next step is to make the author's name and photo appear with a fun bounce effect.

Select **PhotoA** and **AuthorName** by holding down the **Command** key while clicking each object.

With the behavior panel still open, select the **Start** behavior, and add a **Show** action by clicking the + button next to the Action Sequence label.

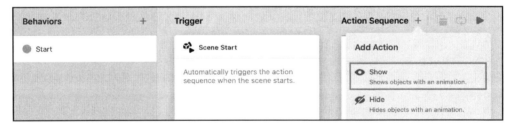

Reality Composer adds a new Show action to the action sequence, assigning the action to the previously-selected objects.

You're now ready to configure the rest of the action sequence.

Set **Move from Above** for the **Motion Type** so that the objects float down onto the card. Set the **Ease Type** to **Ease In** to let the movement decelerate as it gets closer to the card. Set the **Style** to **Basic** and the **Distance** to **30 cm**. This moves the objects starting from 30 cm above the card.

Playtest the action sequence. You'll see the photo with the author's name appear and fall onto the card.

Adding an Emphasize action

To add some pizazz to the sequence, you'll make the photo and name bounce once they hit the card using an **Emphasize** action.

Select the **PhotoA** and **AuthorName** objects by holding down the **Command** key while clicking each object.

Next, click the + button next to the Action Sequence label to add a new action, then select the **Emphasize** action.

Finally, set the **Motion Type** to **Flip** and the **Style** to **Basic**, which will make the objects perform a basic flip animation after they fall.

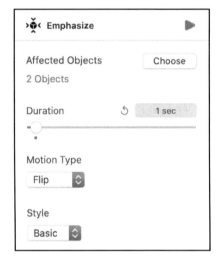

Play the scene to test the state of the action sequence. The photo and name fall from above then do a cool little bounce flip.

Adding a Play Sound action

To take this experience to the next level, you'll add sound into the mix.

This time, select **PhotoA**, then add a **Play Sound** action to the action sequence.

When you add a Play Sound action to an action sequence, you don't want to play the same sound effect from multiple objects. Instead, you assign the effect to a single object in the scene.

Reality Composer comes with a library of commonly-used sounds; you'll use these sounds in this scene.

Set the **Audio Clip** to **Cork Pop FX 01.caf** and leave **Triggered while Running** as **Ignore**.

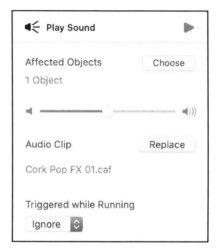

Play the scene and you'll see the author's photo and name fall onto the card, do a quick bounce flip animation, then finish with a nice pop sound effect. Each action completes before the next action starts — hence the name "action sequence".

Grouping actions

Although everything is working properly, something feels a bit off. The last Play Sound action that makes the pop sound feels out of sync with the animation sequence. It would be much better if that effect plays when the objects perform the bounce and flip animation.

Reality Composer has a solution to this problem known as **Grouped Actions**, which let multiple actions play at the same time.

Click and drag the last **Play Sound** action on top of the **Emphasize** action. The Emphasize action window will turn blue, indicating the action on top will be grouped with it.

When you play the scene now, each action waits for the previous action to complete before it plays. The grouped actions play in sync, but the next action in the sequence waits for the longest action in the group to complete first.

Showing the buttons

Fantastic, the photo and text reveal looks great, especially with that nice little pop sound at the end. The next step is to show the buttons.

With the **Start** behavior selected, select **BioButton** and then add another **Show** action to the entire sequence. Change the **Duration** to **0.25 sec** to keep the animation short and sweet. Set the **Motion Type** to **Move from Right** so the button appears from the right side of the card.

Set the **Ease Type** to **Ease InOut** for smooth acceleration and deceleration. Set the **Style** to **Basic** and the **Distance** to **10 m**.

You want that animation to make a pop sound, too, but only once the button has slid into place. To make that happen, select **BioButton**, add a **Play Sound** action, then set the **Audio Clip** to **Cork Pop FX 02.caf**.

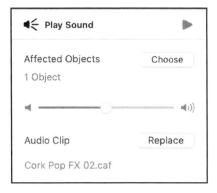

Copying and pasting actions

Instead of duplicating the same actions for the AuthorButton and ContactButton objects, there's a shortcut to use — good old copy and paste!

Select the second-to-last **Show** action in the **Start** behavior action sequence, which will turn blue to indicate that you've selected it. Now, press **Command-C** to copy the selected action to the clipboard.

Select the last **Play Sound** action then press **Command-V** to paste the action from the clipboard.

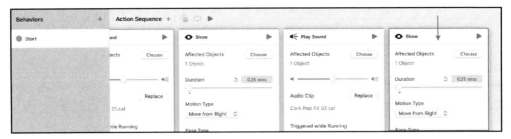

The action will paste after the currently-selected action. In this case, it'll be the last action in the sequence.

Assigning actions to objects

One issue you need to resolve with that newly-pasted action is that it's still assigned to BioButton, so you'll need to re-assign it to AuthorButton.

Click **Choose** on the **Show** action, then click the **BioButton** object to unselect it. Now, click the **AuthorButton** object to select that object instead.

After you've made your selection, click **Done** to finalize the assignment.

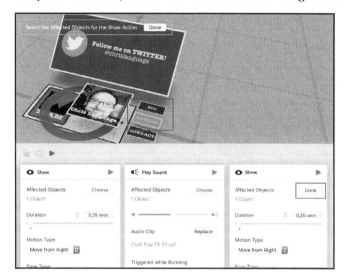

Excellent! The AuthorButton now performs the same action as the BioButton.

Completing the Start behavior

At this point, you're nearly done with the entire Start behavior sequence. Best of all, you now have all the knowledge you need to complete it on your own.

Here are the steps to complete the behavior action sequence:

- **Copy** the **Play Sound** action for the **BioButton**.
- **Paste** it at the **end** of the action sequence.
- **Re-assign** the action to the **AuthorButton** object.
- **Copy** the **Show** action for the **BioButton**.

- **Paste** it at the **end** of the action sequence.

- **Re-assign** the action to the **ContactButton** object.

- **Copy** the **Play Sound** action for the **BioButton**.

- **Paste** it at the **end** of the action sequence.

- **Re-assign** the action to the **ContactButton** object.

Phew! The Start behavior is finally done. It now includes the following actions:

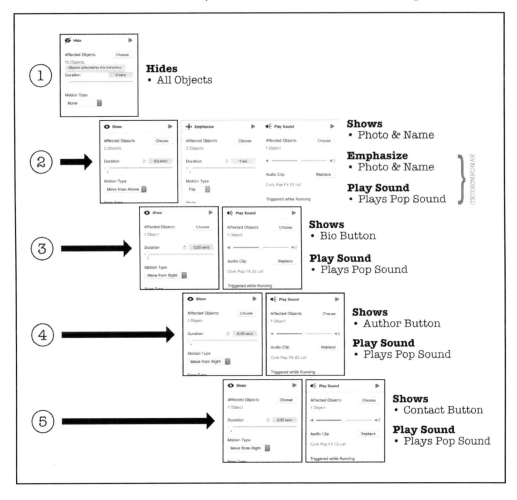

Here's the full action sequence from beginning to end:

1. Hide all of the objects.
2. The author's photo and name fall onto the card, then do a bounce and flip while playing a pop sound.
3. The Bio button slides in from the right then plays a pop sound.
4. The Author button slides in from the right and plays another pop sound.
5. The Contact button slides in from the right then plays a final pop sound.

Adding custom behaviors

Your next step is to make the buttons interactive. When the user taps a button, it flips with a sound effect and makes a related information page appear.

Start by creating a new **Custom Behavior** and renaming it **BioButton_Tap**.

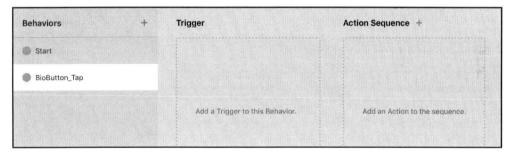

Now that you have a new, empty behavior, you need to add a trigger and an action sequence.

Adding a trigger

To add a trigger to the custom behavior, first select **BioButton**, then click **Add a Trigger to this Behavior** on the behavior. Finally, select the **Tap** trigger.

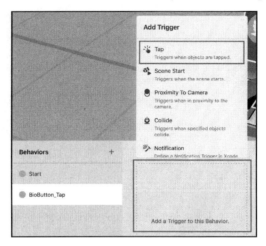

You've now added a Tap trigger to the behavior and assigned it to BioButton. Now, when the user taps on BioButton, it triggers BioButton_Tap's action sequence.

Adding button interactions

Before you can reveal the information pages when the user taps a button, you need to ensure none are visible to start with. To do this, select **BioPage**, **AuthorPage1**, **AuthorPage2** and **ContactPage**, then add a **Hide** action. Set the **Duration** to **0 sec** to instantly hide the pages. Set **Motion Type** to **None**.

Next, you want to emphasize the button to show that the user tapped it. With **BioButton** still selected, add an **Emphasize** action and a **Play Sound** action, and group them together. Set the **Duration** to **1 sec** and the **Motion Type** to **Flip**. Set the **Audio Clip** to **Lighter Click FX.caf**.

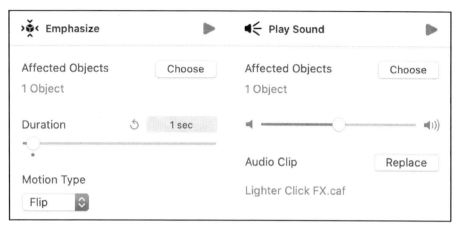

BioButton will now do a cool flip while making a click sound.

Next, it's time to reveal the Bio page. Select **BioPage**, and add **Show** and **Play Sound** actions. Then, group these actions so that they play in sync. Set the **Duration** to **0.1 secs**, the **Motion Type** to **Scale** and the **Ease Type** to **None**. Finally, pick **Cork Pop FX 03.caf** for the **Audio Clip**.

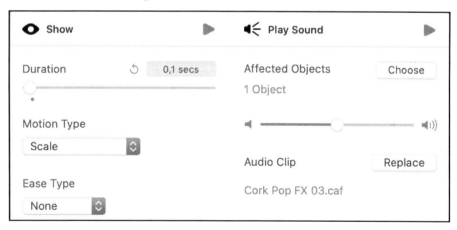

When you playtest the scene now, you'll be able to tap the Bio button,. It will do a cool flip before revealing the Bio page on top of the card.

The scene is slowly but surely coming to life!

Duplicating behaviors

You've done most of the difficult work, but there are a few loose ends left to tie up. The other two buttons still need some action!

Instead of building all of the other behaviors from scratch, you'll use a shortcut. You'll duplicate the behaviors you've already created for the remaining buttons.

Right-click the **BioButton_Tap** behavior to open the context menu, then select **Duplicate**.

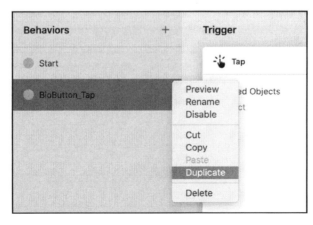

This creates a duplicate behavior containing the same action sequence.

Rename the behavior **AuthorButton_Tap** and re-assign the **Tap** trigger to **AuthorButton**.

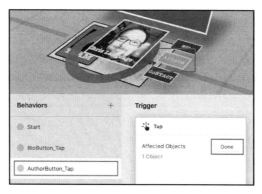

Great, now this action sequence triggers when the user clicks the Author button.

Re-assign the next **Emphasize** and **Play Sound** actions to **AuthorButton**.

The Author button will now do a flip when the user triggers it.

Finally, re-assign the next **Show** and **Play Sound** actions to **AuthorPage1**.

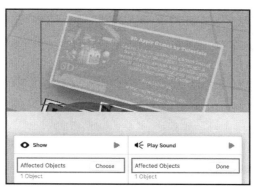

That's it, you've finished the Author button. Now, when you tap that button, it does a quick flip and AuthorPage1 appears.

Follow the same process as before and create a duplicate behavior from **BioButton_Tap**, then re-assign all of the actions to link to the **ContactButton** and the **ContactPage**.

> **Note**: You can find the final project in **final/ARBusinessCard/ARBusinessCard.rcproject**

Challenge yourself

The AR experience is done, but you can add so much more. Challenge yourself to enhance the scene with more fun sounds and animations. What else can you add to make the scene more interesting? Practice the concepts you've learned and explore the other available triggers and actions.

> **Note**: You can find the challenge project in **challenge/ARBusinessCard/ARBusinessCard.rcproject**. It contains a few more behaviors that make the pages interactive, and it even allows you to page through multiple pages. It also has a fun little tweet sound for the contact information.

Key points

That's it! You've finished the chapter and created a cool AR Business Card experience to show your friends.

Here are some of the key points from this chapter:

- **Behaviors**: You now know what a behavior is and that it consists of a trigger and an action sequence.

- **Triggers**: You learned what a trigger is and how it defines the event requirements for a behavior to activate. You also learned about the available triggers and how to use the Tap trigger.

- **Action Sequence**: You know what an action sequence is and how to create multiple sequenced and grouped actions to make things happen exactly when you want them to. You also learned about the available actions and played with Show, Emphasize and Play Sound.

- **Assigning Triggers and Actions**: Now, you know that you assign triggers and actions to objects within the scene.

- **Copy, Paste and Duplicate**: Don't forget that you can copy, paste and duplicate actions and behaviors to reduce your workload. The only thing you need to do is re-assign the actions.

Enjoy making your very own AR Business Card experiences. See you in the next chapter, where you'll go from 2D Image anchors to 3D Object anchors!

Section III: Reality Composer & Object Tracking

In this section, you'll add another dimension with Object tracking. Using object anchors, you'll augment a physical toy truck with interactive buttons that will reveal some fun facts about its real-world counterpart.

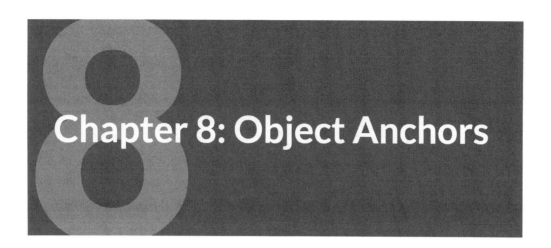

Chapter 8: Object Anchors

In this chapter, you'll learn about object anchors. Object anchors are like 2D image anchors with an added third dimension. To understand how to use object anchors, you'll augment a physical toy truck with interactive buttons that will reveal some fun facts about its real-world counterpart.

Crafting a toy truck

For this project, you'll need a physical object that you can use to create an object model. Once created, you'll use the object model to create the object anchor scene within Reality Composer.

As it turns out, physically attaching a toy truck to this book wasn't possible. But don't worry, we found a solution.

FoldUpToys offers a massive collection of foldable paper toys, and you'll use one of them for this tutorial. Follow this link and see for yourself: https://bit.ly/395UELW

Download the **Tesla Cybertruck** project and print the blueprint.

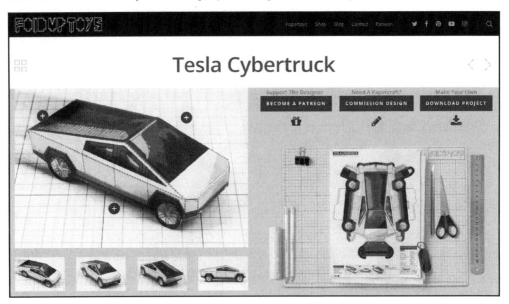

With your printout in hand, grab your scissors and glue — it's time to build yourself a paper truck!

Depending on the level of your crafting skills, your paper truck will look something like this:

What a beauty! Ready for a test drive, so to speak?

What are object anchors?

Reality Composer offers another anchor type known as an **object anchor**. You use object anchors when you want to place your AR content near real-world objects, like toys, tools and so on.

First, you need to create a 3D scan of the real-world object. You then store that scanned data within an .arobject file, which you use as the input for the Reality Composer project.

Reality Composer automatically detects real-world objects based on the scanned data you provide. Once it detects a suitable object, it anchors your AR content to it.

Installing the 3D object scanner

Before you can do anything, you need to install **ARKit Scanner** on your iPhone. You'll use this app to create 3D scans of physical objects.

Unfortunately, ARKit Scanner isn't available on the App Store, so you'll need to download the source code, compile it, and then install it onto your iPhone.

Start by downloading the source code from https://apple.co/32uF8qF.

In addition to the source code, you'll find information about Scanning and Detecting 3D Objects with ARKit. For now, you're only interested in the download.

You'll see the following page:

Click the **Download** button to download the source code for ARKit Scanner.

A zip file named **ScanningAndDetecting3DObjects.zip** will download. Once it's done, extract the contents to a destination of your choice.

You'll see a folder named **ScanningAndDetecting3DObjects**. Within that folder, you'll find an Xcode project named **ScanningApp.xcodeproj**.

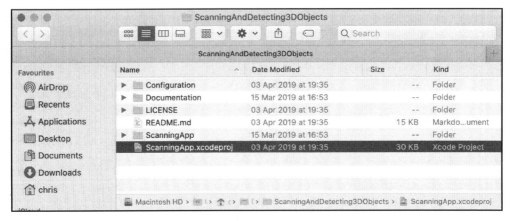

Open **ScanningApp.xcodeproj** in Xcode.

In the Project navigator, select the root **ScanningApp**, then update the **Signing & Capabilities** with your team's information. Connect your iPhone to your Mac and build the app to your iPhone.

You now have ARKit Scanner installed on your device, and you're ready to scan.

Preparing for 3D object scanning

For the data to represent the target object well, you need a good scan. To get the best scan possible, follow these guidelines for preparing your physical environment:

- **Lighting Intensity**: You should light the object with an illuminance of 250 to 400 lux.

- **Lighting Direction**: Light the object from all directions, casting as few shadows as possible.

- **Lighting Temperature**: Provide a light temperature similar to that of daylight, which is around 6,500 kelvin. Avoid warm or colored lights.

- **Background**: For the best results, place the object in front of a textureless, matte, middle-gray background.

To prepare your environment, put four large pieces of white paper on a table, then place the toy truck in the middle. This forms a neutral, textureless background for your target object from all viewable angles. Make sure the room is brightly lit and that the target object is lit from multiple directions.

The resulting environment should look similar to this:

You're ready to scan the object!

Scanning 3D objects

At this point, you've installed the ARKit Scanner app on your iPhone, the environment is set, and the toy truck is ready for you to scan.

Getting started

Start **ARKit Scanner** on your iPhone and follow the step-by-step instructions provided on-screen.

Here's an overview of the process, going from left to right.

The 1st Image:

- The app shows a **Ready to scan** status at the top. This means that tracking is good, and the app is ready to scan the object.
- Start by pointing the phone's camera at the toy truck.

The 2nd Image:

- Move the camera to the left side of the toy truck. Yellow dots, known as feature points, will appear as you move. This means the scanner's starting to detect the object and collect trackable feature points. When the Next button turns blue, ignore it for now. You want to collect as many initial feature points as possible.

The 3rd Image:

- Move the camera to the right side of the toy truck. The scanner will continue to collect feature points.
- The scanner is now ready to create an approximate bounding box around the scanned object based on the feature points it collected.

Refining the bounding box

You're ready to place the approximated bounding box. Tap **Next** to continue.

Continue the process, moving from left to right.

The 1st Image:

- The app shows a **Define bounding box** status at the top. It created an estimated bounding box around the toy truck based on the initial feature points.

- Rotate and align the bounding box with the toy truck. You can use basic gestures. For example, you can rotate the bounding box by twisting two fingers, and you can move it using one finger.

The 2nd Image:

- With one finger, long-press on the front of the bounding box. Four rays will appear to indicate that you can now adjust the front side.

- Still holding your finger on the front side, slide it forward or backward to refine the bounding box so that it covers the entire toy truck.

The 3rd Image:

- Follow the same process as before and adjust all sides of the bounding box. Make sure the toy truck is fully covered by the bounding box — from back to front, from top to bottom, and from side to side. Also, make sure it's nicely centered.

> **Note**: While adjusting the sides of the bounding box, you'll see a pop-up at the top showing its exact width, height and length.

Scanning all the sides

Once you're sure that the bounding box fully covers the toy truck, tap **Scan** to continue.

Continue the scanning process, going from left to right.

The 1st Image:

- The app shows a **Scan (%)** status at the top. This indicates the current completed scanned percentage, which will increase as you scan all sides.

- Start with the top and move the camera over it until that part of the box turns yellow. This indicates you've completed that area of the scan. Notice that the scan percentage increases after each completed area.

- Continue to scan the entire top side. The whole side will turn light yellow when you've completed the side.

The 2nd Image:

- Move to the right side and follow the same process, making sure you move the camera until the side turns yellow.

- Continue to scan the entire right side. It will turn light yellow once done.

The 3rd Image:

- Move to the front side and follow the process again until the side turns yellow.

- Continue to scan the left and back sides until you've completed 100% of the scan.

Adjusting the origin point

Once you've scanned 100% of the object, the scanner will automatically finish and place an estimated origin point on the object.

You now need to adjust the origin point until it's grounded and in the center of the scanned object. Again, you'll start with the left image and move right.

The 1st Image:

- Move to the left side of the toy truck, then move the origin point until it looks like it's in the center of the object. You can push and pull each axis by pulling on the ball-points. **Green** is the **Y-Axis**, **Red** is the **X-Axis** and **Blue** is the **Z-Axis**.

The 2nd Image:

- Move over the front side and continue to adjust the origin point until it's positioned in the middle.

The 3rd Image:

- Move over the right side and continue to adjust origin until it feels perfect.
- Repeat this process while moving around the toy truck from all possible viewing angles.

Once you're happy with the origin point, tap **Test** to continue.

> **Note**: If you have a virtual model of the object you're scanning in USDZ format, you can load the model and preview it by tapping **Load Model**. You won't do that in this tutorial, however.

Testing and improving 3D scans

Now that the scanning process is complete, the only thing left to do is to test the object model.

You should test the detection from different angles. Move the truck to different environments and see if ARKit Scanner detects it there, too.

The 1st Image:

- First, do a basic test from one angle. A notification will appear once ARKit Scanner successfully detects the object. **Detected after** indicates how long it took to recognize the object. Anything less than one second is acceptable.

The 2nd Image:

- Now, move to a different angle. You should see another notification that ARKit Scanner detected the object successfully. Great!

The 3rd Image:

- Turn the light on with the toggle button at the bottom-left. Continue testing from various angles to make sure shadows didn't cause any issues with the scan.

Ok, great, you've scanned the object and tested the results. If the detection took too long, or the recognition wasn't consistent, you should re-scan the object.

When you're done, store the scanned data by tapping **Merge Scans…** at the top-left.

When asked to **Merge another scan**, select **Merge New Scan....** This will store your current scanned data and start a new scanning process. Simply follow the previous instructions to create another scan.

Once you complete the new scan, it will automatically merge with the previous one.

You'll see an on-screen notification that the merge was successful. Multiple scans improve the overall quality of the object model. When testing, you'll see an improved detection time.

Exporting AR objects

At last, you've scanned your object, tested the scan and even improved the model by merging multiple scans. Your next step is to save the scanned data as an **ARObject**.

Tap the **Share** button at the bottom, then AirDrop the **.arobject file** to your Mac.

Once the file finishes copying to your Mac, rename it **TeslaCybertruck.arobject**.

You now have an ARObject reference file ready to go. The only thing left to do now is to create the AR experience.

Creating object anchors

You should be familiar with this part by now, so instead of boring you with the details, we've supplied a ready-made AR experience. All you need to do is add your freshly-created ARObject file.

Open **starter/TeslaCybertruck.rcproject** in RealityComposer.

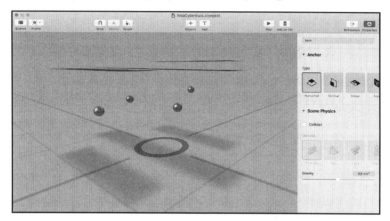

It's a very basic AR experience with four interactive spheres that show some interesting facts about the toy truck. Spend a few minutes playtesting the experience within RealityComposer.

Currently, the experience uses a **Horizontal Anchor**. Change it to use an **Object Anchor** instead.

Once that's done, click **Choose** next to the AR Object Asset label and import the AR object file from **starter/resources/TeslaCybertruck.arobject**.

Click **Import** to complete the process.

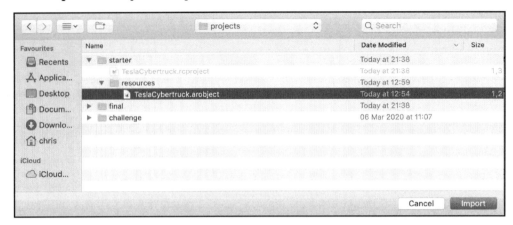

You've now imported and set your scanned AR object file. You'll see a yellow cube with an image of the scanned object on it.

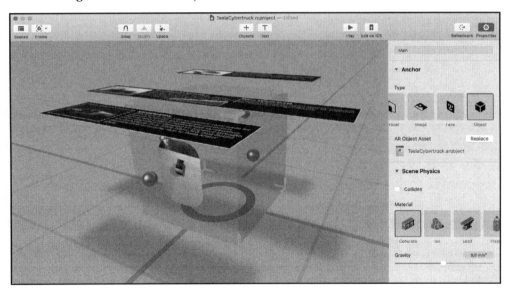

You've successfully created an Object Anchored AR experience.

Export the AR experience by selecting **File ▸ Export ▸ Export Project…**. Rename the experience **TeslaCybertruck.reality**, then click **Export** to complete the process.

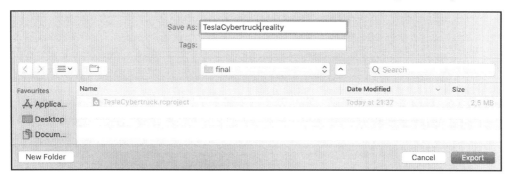

AirDrop the **TeslaCybertruck.reality** file to your iPhone and test it.

The scene recognizes the toy truck and displays four spheres around it. Tapping a sphere reveals some interesting facts about the toy truck.

Key points

Congratulations, you've finished this chapter, and you've successfully created an Object Anchor AR Experience.

Here are some of the key things you achieved in this chapter:

- **Object Anchors**: You learned about Object Anchors, which allow you to anchor AR content to physical objects in the real world.
- **ARKit Scanner**: You compiled and installed ARKit Scanner onto your iPhone so you can scan your own physical objects.
- **Scanning Preparation**: You learned how to prepare your environment so that you can scan physical objects. You now know the importance of lighting intensity, direction and temperature.
- **Scanning Objects**: You went through the process of scanning a 3D object. First, you defined a basic bounding box, then you scanned the object, and finally, you adjusted the origin point.
- **Improving Scans**: You improved a scan by merging multiple scanned data to create an even better AR object.
- **AR Object files**: You exported an AR object file from ARKit Scanner, then imported it as reference for an Object Anchor AR experience.

Take a well deserved breather. See you in the next chapter where you get to learn more about creating your own AR apps with RealityKit.

Section IV: RealityKit & Face Tracking

In this section, you'll learn about RealityKit and face tracking. You'll create a SnapChat-like face filter app with SwiftUI that lets you mockup your face with funny props. You'll also create an animated mask that you can control with your eyes, brows and mouth.

Chapter 9: RealityKit

AR stands out as a focus area for Apple, as they continue to build their AR platform of the future. Thanks to AR Quick Look, AR has become extremely accessible and is now deeply integrated into iOS, macOS and tvOS.

Creating immersive AR experiences has historically been difficult, requiring a vast amount of skill and knowledge. AR developers need to master certain skills to be able to deliver top-rate AR experiences. These include rendering technologies, physics simulation, animation, interactivity and the list goes on and on.

Thankfully, that all changed with the introduction of **RealityKit**.

RealityKit

With RealityKit in your toolbox, creating AR experiences has never been easier.

In this section, you'll learn all about RealityKit and face tracking. You'll create a SnapChat-like face filter app with SwiftUI called **AR Funny Face**, where you get to mock up your face with funny props. You'll also create an animated mask that you can control with your eyes, brows and mouth.

What is RealityKit?

RealityKit is a new Swift framework that Apple introduced at WWDC 2019. Apple designed it from the ground up with AR development in mind. Its main purpose is to help you build AR apps and experiences more easily. Thanks to the awesome power of Swift, RealityKit delivers a high-quality framework with a super simple API.

RealityKit is a high-quality rendering technology capable of delivering hyper-realistic, physically-based graphics with precise physics simulation and collisions against the real-world environment. It does all of the heavy lifting for you, right out of the box. It makes your content look as good as possible while fitting seamlessly into the real world. It's impressive feature list includes skeletal animations, realistic shadows, lights, reflections and post-processing effects.

Are you ready to give it a try? Open RealityKit and take a look at what's inside.

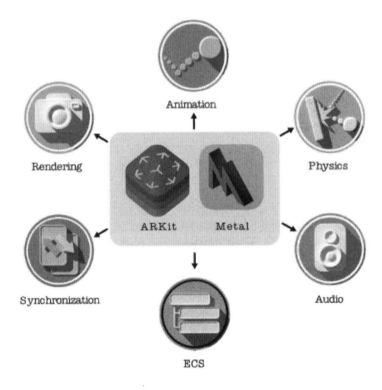

At its core, you'll find many of Apple's other frameworks, but the ones doing most of the work are ARKit and Metal.

Here's a breakdown of RealityKit's coolest features:

- **Rendering**: RealityKit offers a powerful new physically-based renderer built on top of Metal, which is fully optimized for all Apple devices.

- **Animation**: It has built-in support for Skeletal animation and Transform-based animation. So, if you want, you can animate a zombie or you can move, scale and rotate objects with various easing functions.

- **Physics**: With a powerful physics engine, RealityKit lets you throw anything at it — pun intended! You can adjust real-world physics properties like mass, drag and restitution, allowing you to fine-tune collisions.

- **Audio**: Spacial audio understanding and automatic listener configuration let you attach sound effects to 3D objects. You can then track those sounds, making them sound realistic based on their position in the real world.

- **ECS**: From a coding perspective, RealityKit enforces the *Entity Component System* design pattern to build objects within the world.

- **Synchronization**: The framework has built-in support for networking, designed for collaborative experiences. It even offers automatic synchronization of entities between multiple clients.

Enough talk, it's time to dive into some code!

Creating a RealityKit project

Now that you have some understand about RealityKit's features, you'll create your first RealityKit project. Launch Xcode and get ready to create a new Augmented Reality App project from scratch.

> **Note**: If you'd rather skip creating the project from scratch and use the starter project instead — which also includes the app icons — you can load it from **starter/ARFunnyFace.xcodeproj**. Feel free to skip to the next section.

Choose the following template **iOS ▸ Augmented Reality App**:

Click **Next** to continue. Set the **Product Name** to **ARFunnyFace** and fill in the rest of the information.

Xcode now has a newly-added **RealityKit** option under **Content Technologies**. Make sure to choose **SwiftUI** for your **User Interface**:

Click **Next** and save the project somewhere safe. Xcode will continue to generate the project for you, with the end result looking like this:

Before doing anything else, build and run the project to give it a quick try before taking a look at what Xcode generated.

Wow, out of the box your app is already doing quite a bit. It's requesting access to the camera, it's detecting horizontal surfaces and it has proper environmental lighting and reflections. And where did that smooth-looking cube come from? You didn't have to write one single line of code to achieve all that. Nice!

Well, you'll be even more impressed when you look at what's inside the project.

Reviewing the project

At first glance within the project, you'll notice the usual suspects — but there are a few new things, too:

- **AppDelegate.swift**: This is the app's starting point.

- **ContentView.swift**: Since this is a SwiftUI-based app, the user interface is defined here. From the preview, you can see that the UI is currently a blank slate. Internally, the ContentView constructs an ARView that loads and presents the scene located within the **Experience.rcproject** Reality Composer project. It's also important to point out that this file updates ARView.

- **Experience.rcproject**: This is a **Reality Composer** project, which is essentially a 3D scene that contains the box and the box anchor you used in the previous step.

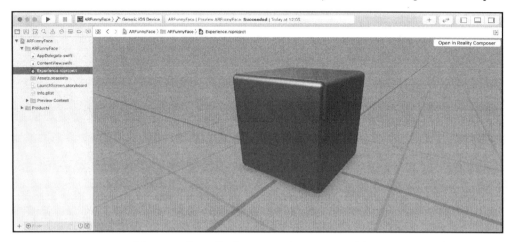

- **Assets.xcassets**: This contains all of your project assets, like images and app icons.

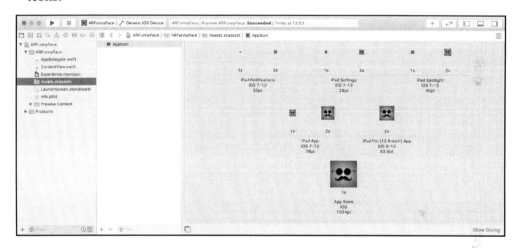

- **LaunchScreen.storyboard**: Here, you'll find the UI the user sees while your app is launching.

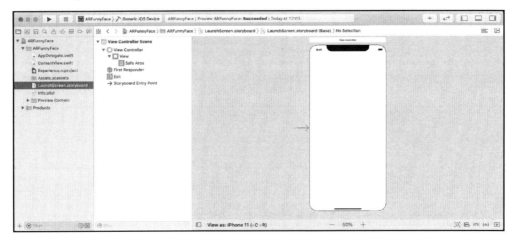

- **Info.plist**: Contains the app's basic configuration settings. Note that there's already a **Camera Usage Description** property, you just need to change it to something more appropriate for your app. This allows the app to request access to the camera from the user, which you need to deliver the AR experience through the camera view.

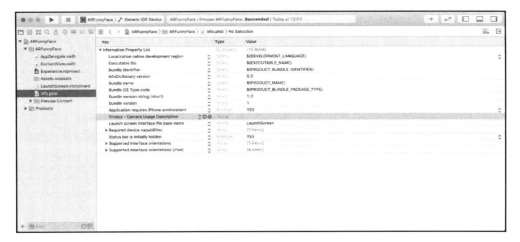

RealityKit API components

Now, take a look at a few main components that form parts of the RealityKit API.

Here's an example of a typical structure containing all of the important elements:

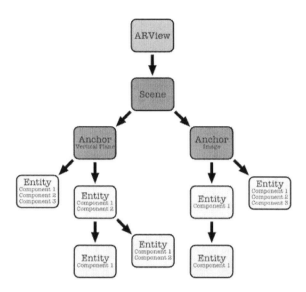

- **ARView**: The `ARView` sits at the core of any RealityKit experience, taking responsibility for all of the heavy lifting. It comes with full gesture support, allowing you to attach gestures to entities. It also handles the post-processing camera effects, which is very similar to the effects you saw in AR Quick Look.

- **Scene**: Think of this as the container for all of your entities.

- **Anchor**: RealityKit exposes ARKit's available anchors — plane, face, body, image and object — as first-class citizens. Anchors form the local root for entity structures. Note that content attached to an anchor will stay hidden until you successfully identify it and connect it to the real world.

- **Entity**: You can picture each element of the virtual content in a scene as an *entity* — the basic building block of your experience. You can establish a tree-like hierarchical structure by parenting entities to other entities.

- **Components**: Entities consist of different types of *components*. These components give the entities specific features and functionality, like how they look, how they respond to collisions and how they react to physics.

Building the UI with SwiftUI

When you created the app, you selected SwiftUI for the user interface. Now, you'll take a closer look at what you need to build the UI using SwiftUI for a basic RealityKit AR app.

The UI is very simple, and it requires only three basic buttons: **Next**, **Previous** and **Shutter**.

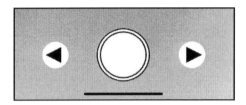

You'll use the Next and Previous buttons to switch between various AR scenes, while the Shutter button will take the all-important selfie. But your first order of business is to learn how to track the active prop by implementing the Next and Previous buttons.

Tracking the active prop

Your AR experience is going to contain multiple scenes with various props to make your pictures funnier. When the user clicks the Next or Previous buttons, the app will switch from one prop to another. You'll implement that functionality now.

Open **ContentView.swift** and define a variable to keep track of the active prop by adding the following line of code at the top of `ContentView`:

```
@State var propId: Int = 0
```

`@State` indicates that SwiftUI will manage `propId`'s storage. When the state value changes, the view invalidates its appearance, which will recompute the body. State variables are the *single source of truth* for the view.

Add the following line of code to the top of `ARViewContainer`:

```
@Binding var propId: Int
```

`@Binding` creates a two-way connection between the property that stores the data and the view that changes and displays the data.

You now need to pass in `propId` as a parameter to `ARViewContainer()` to clear the error and complete the binding process.

Find the following line of code within `ContentView`:

```
return ARViewContainer().edgesIgnoringSafeArea(.all)
```

Replace it with the following code block:

```
// 1
ZStack(alignment: .bottom) {
  // 2
  ARViewContainer(propId: $propId).edgesIgnoringSafeArea(.all)
  // 3
  HStack {
  }
}
```

Take a look at what's happening here:

1. To overlay the UI buttons on the AR view, you place the elements into a `ZStack`.

2. You provide the `$propId` as a parameter for `ARViewContainer()`, completing the binding process. So when the value of `propId` changes, it invalidates the `ARView`.

3. Finally, you stack the buttons horizontally within an `HStack`.

Great! You've now created a variable to keep track of the active prop. You'll update this variable when the user presses the Next and Previous buttons to swap between the various scenes within the Reality Composer experience.

> **Note**: This will momentarily cause a compiler error. Ignore this for now, you'll fix the problem in the next section.

Adding buttons

The buttons all use images. So next, you'll add the required images to the project by dragging and dropping all the image files from **starter/resources/images** into **Assets.xcassets**.

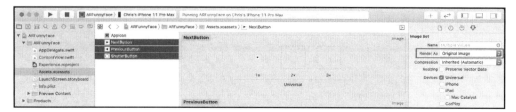

Under the **Properties** panel, be sure to set **Image Set ▸ Render As** to **Original Image**. Otherwise, the images will display with a blue highlight.

Now, you can reference these images within **ContentView.swift**.

Starting with the Previous button, add the following line of code inside the `HStack`:

```
Button(action: {
  self.propId = self.propId <= 0 ? 0 : self.propId - 1
}) {
  Image("PreviousButton").clipShape(Circle())
}
```

This creates a `Button` view with a defined action (and clears the error). When the user presses the button, the value of `propId` decreases by 1, but the value will never decrease below `0`.

You also place an `Image` view within the `Button` view, using the image reference named `PreviousButton`, which you clip into a circular shape.

As you did with the Previous button, add the following line of code for the Shutter button:

```
Button(action: {
  //self.TakeSnapshot()
}) {
  Image("ShutterButton").clipShape(Circle())
}
```

This code works nearly the same in the Previous button. The only difference is that the action makes a call to a function named `self.TakeSnapShot()`, which you'll define at a later stage. Leave it commented out for now.

Finally, add the following code for the Next button:

```
Button(action: {
    self.propId = self.propId >= 2 ? 2 : self.propId + 1
}) {
    Image("NextButton").clipShape(Circle())
}
```

This also operates like the Previous button. The difference is that the action will *increase* the value of the `propId` by 1, but the value can't exceed 2.

The end result should look like the preview on the right:

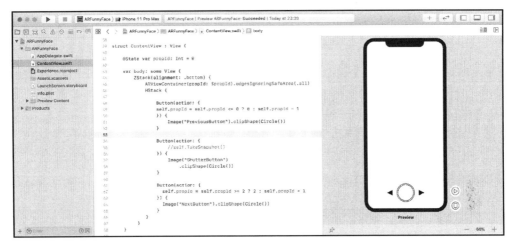

To space the buttons more evenly, add a `Spacer()` before, between and after each button:

```
Spacer()
```

There should be a total of four spacers when you're done. This spreads the UI elements evenly across the `HStack`.

The final result will look like this:

Excellent, you've now defined all of the UI elements. Now it's time to add some functionality to the Shutter button.

Taking selfies

What good is an AR face mockup app if you can't use it to take selfies?

For quick access to the `ARView`, add the following declaration to the top of **ContentView.swift**:

```
var arView: ARView!
```

Find the following line of code within `ARViewContainer`:

```
let arView = ARView(frame: .zero)
```

Then simply remove the `let` keyword so it looks like this:

```
arView = ARView(frame: .zero)
```

This initializes the quick-accessible `arView` variable instead of a local one.

Next, add the following helper function to `ContentView`:

```
func TakeSnapshot() {
  // 1
  arView.snapshot(saveToHDR: false) { (image) in
```

```
    // 2
    let compressedImage = UIImage(
      data: (image?.pngData())!)
    // 3
    UIImageWriteToSavedPhotosAlbum(
      compressedImage!, nil, nil, nil)
  }
}
```

Wow, is that all it takes? Here's a breakdown:

1. This takes a snapshot of the current `ARView`, providing `image` as a result.

2. Here, you create a compressed version of the image to reduce the image size.

3. Finally, you save the compressed image into the photo's album.

Don't forget to uncomment the call to `TakeSnapshot()` in the action for the Shutter button:

```
self.TakeSnapshot()
```

Fantastic! When the user chooses the Shutter button now, the app takes a snapshot of `ARView` and stores the image in the photo's album.

Requesting access to the camera and photos

You're not done just yet. You still need to make sure the app asks for access to the camera and the photo's album.

Open **Info.plist** and find **Privacy — Camera Usage Description**. Set the value to **Access required for AR experience**.

When the user starts the app for the first time, the app now requests access to the camera.

Add a new key by clicking the Plus Sign button next to the current key.

For the new key, select **Privacy — Photo Library Additions Usage Description**. Set the value to **Access required to save selfies**.

This will request access to the photo library when the user takes a selfie.

Finally, reap the fruits of your labor and do a quick build and run to test the app.

The app starts and requests access to the camera. The scene loads and presents the cube. The glorious UI displays on top of the `ARView`. When you select the Shutter button, it requests access to the photo library, then it takes and stores a snapshot.

For now, the Previous and Next buttons don't do much, but you'll deal with that in the next chapter.

Key points

You've reached the end of this chapter. To recap some of the key takeaways:

- You now know about Apple's latest and greatest RealityKit framework, designed for AR. It helps reduce the complexities AR developers face.

- Reality Composer is tightly integrated into Xcode, which generates companion code that gives you strongly-typed access to your virtual scenes and content.

- Creating a UI with SwiftUI for RealityKit apps is super easy, now that you know how.

Where to go from here?

There's much more content about RealityKit waiting for you from WWDC 2019. I highly recommend you check out the following:

- Information about RealityKiy and Reality Composer — https://apple.co/2OYxIsG

- WWDC's video on RealityKit & Reality Composer — https://apple.co/2GP6iyI

See you in the next chapter, where you'll continue building your AR Funny Face app and learn more about face anchors.

Chapter 10: Face Anchors

This chapter continues from the point where the previous one left off. Thanks to SwiftUI, the AR Funny Face app now sports a very basic UI. In this chapter, you'll continue to focus on that facial recognition component by using **face anchors** in RealityKit.

You'll also get to build some funny scenes with these crazy props:

A humongous pair of sunglasses, a glass eyeball and one epic mustache. With these cool props at one's disposal, the AR Funny Face app is off to a great start.

> **Note**: Feel free to continue with your own final project from the previous chapter. If you skipped a few things, load the starter project from **starter/ARFunnyFace/ARFunnyFace.xcodeproj** before you continue.

What are face anchors?

Hanging an anchor from one's face sounds extremely painful. Luckily, the type of anchor we're referring to here is an **AR Face Anchor** — undeniably one of the coolest types of anchors available. Thanks to Reality Composer, creating face anchors is super easy.

By using the TrueDepth front-facing camera, face anchors provide information about the user's facial position, orientation, topology and facial expression.

Unfortunately, you can only use face tracking if you have a device equipped with a TrueDepth front-facing camera. If the device is Face-Id capable, you're good to go.

When the camera detects a face, an anchor gets added slightly behind the nose in the middle of the head.

Here, the cute monkey head demonstrates how a face anchor is created after a face is detected.

It's also important to know that the anchor uses a right-handed coordinate system measured in meters.

Here's a breakdown of each axis:

- **X-Axis**: The **red** arrow pointing **right** represents this axis.

- **Y-Axis**: The **green** arrow pointing **up** represents this axis.

- **Z-Axis**: The **blue** arrow pointing **forward** represents this axis.

Creating face anchors

It's time to dive into the action and build some face anchor scenes with the provided props.

With the AR Funny Face app project open, select **Experience.rcproject** then select **Open in Reality Composer**.

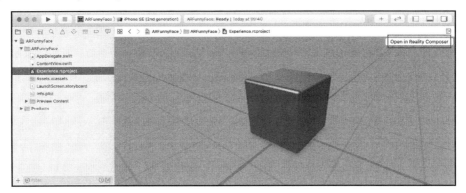

The project opens in Reality Composer with the default scene selected. The scene contains a cube object.

Select the default scene and open the **Properties** panel. Rename the **Scene** to **Eyes**. Change the **Scene Anchor Type** to **Face** and disable the **Scene Physics** by setting **Objects collide with** to **Nothing**. Finally, select the default **Cube** within the scene and delete it.

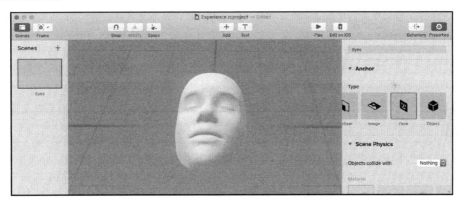

Because you set the **Anchor Type** to **Face**, you'll now see a white face mask in the center of the scene. The mask represents a detected face in scale. The mask serves as a visual guide to know where you can place objects in relation to the detected face.

Add an object to the scene, but select the **Import** option to select a custom object. Find and select **starter/resources/Eyeball.usdz** then select **Import** to complete the process.

This imports a beautiful, shiny glass eyeball into the scene, hiding behind the white mask. Rotate until you can see the eyeball behind the mask. Select it, then open the **Properties** panel.

Rename the object to **Eye_R**, which represents the right eye. Under the **Transform** section, set the **Position** to (X:-3.5cm, Y:4cm, Z:-3cm) and set the **Scale** to 170%.

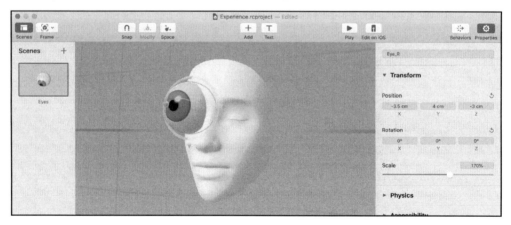

Now, you have a good idea of how the end product will look when you view the scene. You need at least one more eye, though.

With the right eyeball still selected, press **Command-C** then **Command-V** to create a quick copy.

Rename the object to **Eye_L**, which represents the left eye. Under the **Transform** section, set the **Position** to (X:3.5cm, Y:4cm, Z:-3cm) and set the **Scale** to 170%.

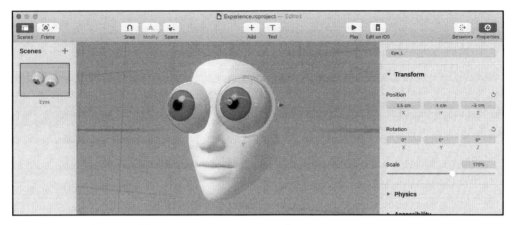

The final result resembles Homer Simpson. Perfect!

Now that the eyes are done, it's time to add the other props.

Creating multiple scenes

To add more props, you have to create multiple scenes within the Reality Composer project. Each scene will house a single facial prop. To switch between the different props, you simply need to switch the different scenes.

That sounds like a great plan, so get to it!

With the **Scenes** panel open, add a new scene to the project by selecting the + button at the top-left of the panel.

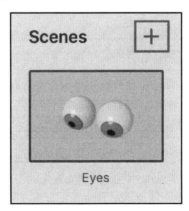

Each scene has its own anchor, so when you create a new scene, you'll need to select an anchor type for it. When asked, choose **Face** as the anchor type and make sure to uncheck **Use template content** to create the scene with no content.

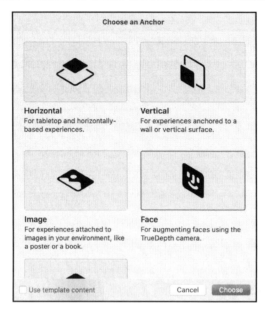

Rename the **Scene** to **Glasses** and set **Objects collide with** to **Nothing**.

Add an object to the scene then **Import** the **starter/resources/Glasses.usdz**.

Rotate the scene until you can see the glasses behind the face mask, then select them and open the **Properties** panel. Under the Transform section, set the **Position** to (X:0cm, Y:6cm, Z:-3cm:). To make the glasses nice and big, set the **Scale** to 140%.

All right Willy Wonka, you're almost done. There's one more prop left to add to the project.

Following the same process as before, make sure the **Scenes** panel is open, then add another scene to the project by clicking the + button at the top-left of the panel.

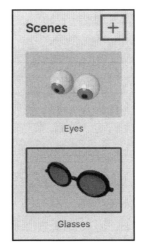

When asked, set the **Anchor Type** to **Face**. Don't forget to make sure you've unchecked **Use template content**.

Rename the scene to **Mustache** and add an object to the scene, then import **starter/resources/Mustache.usdz**.

To wrap things up, rename the object to **Mustache**, set the **Position** to (X:0cm, Y:6.5cm, Z:3cm) and set the **Scale** to 130%.

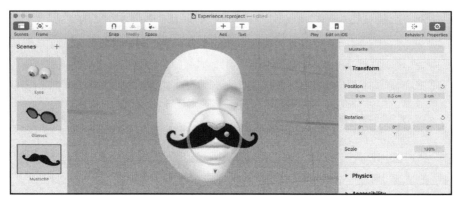

That's it, you're all done. Your Reality Composer project now contains three different face anchor scenes, one for each prop.

Save your changes, close Reality Composer and return to Xcode.

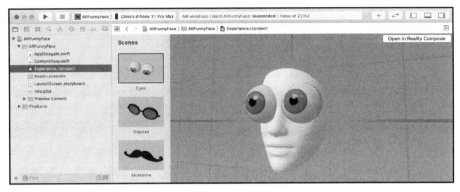

You'll now see your three scenes within Xcode.

Code generation

Reality Composer is tightly integrated into Xcode. When you build the project, Xcode will inspect all the associated Reality files within the project and generate Swift code.

The generated code provides strongly-typed access to all the content within the Reality file. It also provides direct access to invoke triggers for custom actions within your code.

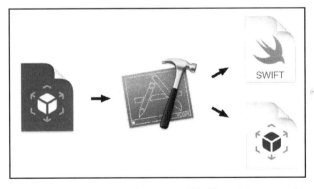

In this case, Xcode generates an **Experience.swift** file with strongly-typed access to the three scenes you created within the Reality file.

Fixing the project

You'll look at the coding side of the project next. When you recompile your project, it generates an error.

That's because you removed the default box scene. The generated **Experience.swift** code no longer has any reference to `Experience.loadBox()`.

Select **ContentView.swift**. You'll add some code to it next.

Find `makeUIView(context:)` and replace its contents with the following block of code:

```
arView = ARView(frame: .zero)
return arView
```

This initializes `arView`. As an added bonus, you just got rid of the code that was causing a compiler error.

Switching to the front-facing camera

When the app starts, you need to manually switch to the front-facing camera. To do that, you'll need a little help from **ARKit**.

ARKit is the technology behind RealityKit; you'll learn more about it later in the book.

Add the following import to the top of **ContentView.swift**:

```
import ARKit
```

Great, now you have low-level access to some additional content.

AR session

Before moving on, you need to learn about the **AR session**, which you can access via `ARView.session`.

The AR session object is the key technology responsible for motion tracking and image processing. It's session-based, so you have to create an AR session instance, then you have to run that session to start the AR tracking process.

AR configuration

Before starting an AR session, you have to create an AR session configuration. You use this configuration to establish the connection between the real world, where your device is, and the virtual 3D world, where your virtual content is.

There are six types of configurations:

- **AROrientationTrackingConfiguration**: Basic three degrees of freedom (3DOF) tracking, which uses the back camera.
- **ARWorldTrackingConfiguration**: Six degrees of freedom (6DOF) tracking, which also tracks people, known images and objects. It uses the back camera.
- **ARBodyTrackingConfiguration**: Tracks human bodies only. It uses the back camera.
- **ARImageTrackingConfiguration**: Tracks known images only, using the back camera.
- **ARObjectScanningConfiguration**: Use this to scan 3D objects you want to track. It uses the back camera.
- **ARFaceTrackingConfiguration**: Tracks faces and facial expressions only. This uses the front camera.

The one you'll use now is `ARFaceTrackingConfiguration`. When you run this configuration, your app will switch to the front-facing camera.

Add the following block of code to `updateView(_:context:)`:

```
// 1
let arConfiguration = ARFaceTrackingConfiguration()
// 2
uiView.session.run(arConfiguration,
  options:[.resetTracking, .removeExistingAnchors])
```

Take a closer look at what you're doing with this code:

1. First, you create a new instance of `ARFaceTrackingConfiguration` within `arConfiguration`. The configuration now contains the necessary information to let the AR session know that you want to start tracking faces.

2. This starts the AR session with the newly-created AR configuration along with a few additional options. `resetTracking` indicates that you want to restart the AR tracking process. `removeExistingAnchors` removes all existing anchors, if there are any.

Switching between multiple scenes

Finally, you need to switch between the three scenes when the user presses the Previous or Next buttons.

Add the following block of code to the bottom of `updateView(:context:)`:

```
switch(propId) {

  case 0: // Eyes
    let arAnchor = try! Experience.loadEyes()
    uiView.scene.anchors.append(arAnchor)
    break

  case 1: // Glasses
    let arAnchor = try! Experience.loadGlasses()
    uiView.scene.anchors.append(arAnchor)
    break

  case 2: // Mustache
    let arAnchor = try! Experience.loadMustache()
    uiView.scene.anchors.append(arAnchor)
    break

  default:
    break
}
```

Every time the user presses Next or Previous, the value of `propId` increases or decreases by 1, which invalidates the scene and makes a call to `updateView(:context:)`. The switch statement then inspects the value of `propId` to switch to the appropriate scene.

First, you initialize `arAnchor` by loading the corresponding anchor scene from `Experience`. Once loaded, you append the anchor to `arView.scene.anchors`, which presents that particular scene in the view.

Testing the app

Finally, you're ready to do your very first build and run. Before you do, connect your physical device to your machine and select it in Xcode.

> **Note**: You will experience compiler issues if you don't connect your physical device to Xcode and select it as the build destination.

Ready to build and run? Go for it!

Excellent, the app started and you can use the Next and Previous buttons to select the different props.

Although it looks kind of cool, there's a small problem — the props get stuck and never go away.

Manually removing anchors

Every time you switch from one scene to another, you load an anchor that appends to `ARView.Scene.anchors`. If you continue adding multiple anchors, you'll end up with multiple props stacked on top of each other.

To solve that problem, you need to manually remove the previously-appended anchors before appending a new one.

Add the following line of code to the top of `updateView(_:context:)`:

```
arView.scene.anchors.removeAll()
```

This removes all the available anchors within `arView.scene.anchors`.

Remember that every time the user selects the Next or Previous button, it invalidates the scene and makes a call to `updateView(_:context:)`. So every time the user switches to a new prop, the app removes the previous prop (face anchor) before appending the new one.

Do another build and run to test the app again.

Excellent, you can now swap between props without any issues.

> **Note**: You can find the final project at **final/ARFunnyFace/ARFunnyFace.xcodeproj**.

Key points

Congratulations, you've reached the end of this chapter and your AR Funny Face app looks great. Take some selfies of yourself and some friends and try the funny props.

Here are some of the key points you covered in this chapter:

- **Face Anchors**: You now have a good idea of what face anchors are and how to use them within your scenes.
- **Creating Face Anchors**: Thanks to Reality Creator, creating face anchors is really easy.
- **Creating Multiple Scenes**: A single Reality Composer can contain multiple scenes, which are really easy to add.
- **Code Generation**: Reality Composer is tightly integrated into Xcode. When compiling, Xcode generates code that provides strongly-typed access to the content of the scenes and objects within the Reality file.
- **AR Session & Configuration**: You learned about AR session and how to create your own AR configurations.
- **Switching Between Scenes**: Finally, you learned how easy it is to switch between multiple scenes within a RealityKit app.

In the next chapter, you'll extend the AR Funny Face app with one more scene, where you get to control a giant robot head with your own facial expressions!

Chapter 11: Facial Blend Shapes

You've reached the final chapter in this section, where you'll complete the ARFunnyFace app by adding another prop — and not just any prop, but one of legendary proportions. Prepare to come face-to-face with the mighty **Green Robot Head**!

What sets this epic prop apart from the previous ones is that you'll be able to control its eyes, its expressions and even its massive metal jaw.

Like a true puppeteer, you'll be able to animate this robot head using your own facial movements and expressions, thanks to facial blend shapes. Awesome!

What are facial blend shapes?

ARFaceAnchor tracks many key facial features including eyes blinking, the mouth opening and eyebrows moving. These key tracking points are known as **blend shapes**.

You can easily use these blend shapes to animate 2D or 3D characters to mimic the user's facial expressions.

Here's an example of a 2D smiley character that animates by tracking the user's eyes and mouth.

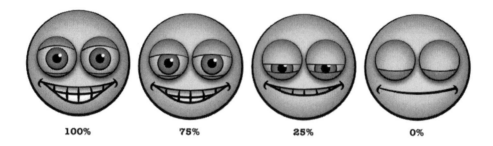

Each key tracking feature is represented by a floating point number that indicates the current position of the corresponding facial feature.

These blend shape values range from **0.0**, indicating a neutral position to **1.0**, indicating the maximum position. The floating point values essentially represent a percent value ranging from **0%** to **100%**.

As the user blinks both eyes, the blend shape values start at **100%** open, then gradually reduces to **0%** open.

The mouth works the same way, starting at **100%** open then reducing to **0%** open.

You use the percentage values to animate the corresponding facial features from a **100%** open position to a **0%** open position — aka, closed.

You can even prerecord the blend shape data, which you can play back at a later time to animate your game characters, for example. Sweet!

Building the robot

Next, it's time to build the Mighty Green Robot head. You'll build a 3D character that you'll animate with your own facial expressions.

Open **starter/ARFunnyFace/ARFunnyFace.xcodeproj** in Xcode, then select **Experience.rcproject** and open it in **Reality Composer**.

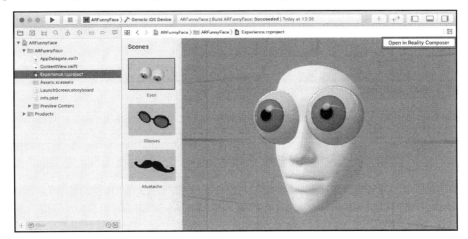

Open the **Scenes** panel and create a new scene that uses a **Face Anchor**. With the **Properties** panel open, rename the scene to **Robot**.

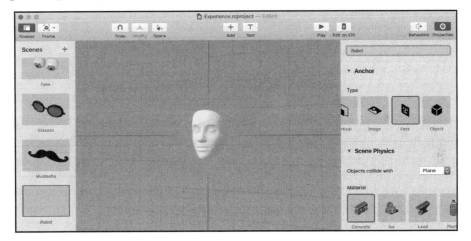

Now, you'll add a **Basic ▸ Capsule** to the **Robot** scene.

Under the **Transform** section, set **Position** to (X:0, Y:0, Z:0), **Rotation** to (X:90°, Y:0°, Z:0°) and leave **Scale** at **100%**.

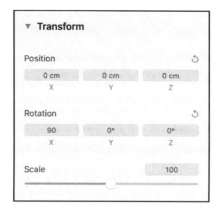

Finally, go to the **Look** section, choose **Matte Paint** for the **Material** and set the **Material Color** to **Black**. Set the **Capsule Diameter** to **18 cm** and the **Height** to **22 cm**.

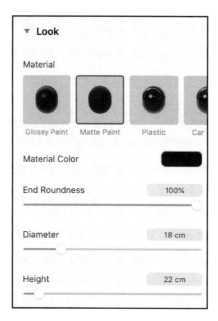

Both the face mask in the scene and the user's face should now be fully obscured.

Now you'll create the rest of the robot head, which consists of four basic parts: a **RobotEye**, a **RobotEyelid**, a **RobotJaw** and a **RobotSkull**.

Import all of these assets into the **Robot** scene from **starter/resources**.

As always, the parts are stacked next to each other when you import them. You'll need to put them in their rightful places.

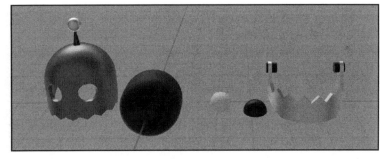

The robot needs two eyes and two eyelids, so create a copy of the **RobotEye** and the **RobotEyeLid**.

Apply the following settings to each element using the data from the table below:

Element	Name	Position	Rotation
RobotSkull	Skull	X: 0cm, Y: -1cm, Z: -2cm	X: -90°, Y: 0°, Z: 0°
RobotEye1	Eye_L	X: 3.2cm , Y: 6cm, Z: -4.7cm	X: 0°, Y: 0°, Z: 0°
RobotEyeLid1	EyeLid_L	X: 3.2cm, Y: 6cm, Z: -4.7cm	X: -120°, Y: 0°, Z: 0°
RobotEye2	Eye_R	X: -3.2cm, Y: 6cm, Z: -4.7cm	X: 0°, Y: 0°, Z: 0°
RobotEyeLid2	EyeLid_R	X: -3.2cm, Y: 6cm, Z: -4.7cm	X: -120°, Y: 0°, Z: 0°
RobotJaw	Jaw	X: 0cm, Y: -1cm, Z: -2cm	X: -100°, Y: 0°, Z: 0°

The result should look like this:

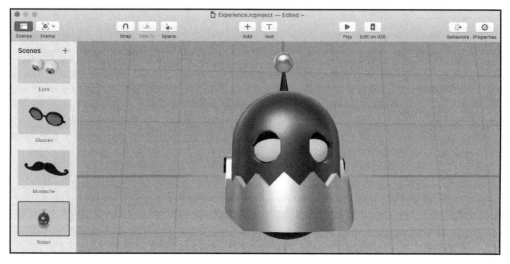

The Mighty Green Robot Head is done! Save all of your changes and close Reality Composer, then jump back to Xcode.

Adding the new robot scene

Now that you've built the Robot scene, you need to update the app so it knows about the additional prop.

Add the following variable to the top of **ContentView.swift**:

```
var robot: Experience.Robot!
```

This gives you quick access to the robot anchor, once you initialize it.

Now, initialize the new variable, robot, at the top of updateUIView(_:context:):

```
robot = nil
```

This makes sure that, if you haven't loaded the anchor, robot is nil. When you inspect the value of robot and it's nil, you know the robot head hasn't been activated.

Next, you need to modify the **Next** button so, when the user selects it, the app increases the propId count to handle four props instead of just three.

Within the body variable, modify the **Next** button action code block to look like this:

```
self.propId = self.propId >= 3 ? 3 : self.propId + 1
```

Great, now the app can select the additional prop, giving it a total of four available props. Now, you just need to cater for this new case in the update.

Add the following case to handle the robot prop in updateUIView(_:context:):

```
case 3: // Robot
  // 1
  let arAnchor = try! Experience.loadRobot()
  // 2
  uiView.scene.anchors.append(arAnchor)
  // 3
  robot = arAnchor
  break
```

Here's how it breaks down:

1. This loads the Robot scene from **Experience.rcproject** and stores it in arAnchor.

2. It then appends arAnchor to the scene anchors.

3. Finally, it stores arAnchor in robot so other parts of the code can use it to get notifications when the robot prop is active. It also provides quick access to all the elements of the robot head.

Now would be a great time to do a quick check to make sure everything still works as intended. Do a quick build and run.

Fantastic! You can select the new prop and, goodness, the Mighty Green Robot head looks so shiny.

Everything is still very static… you'll address that next.

Using the ARSessionDelegate protocol

To animate the robot's eyelids and jaw, you need to update their positions and rotations as `ARFaceAnchor` tracks the user's facial expressions in real time. You'll use a class that conforms to `ARSessionDelegate` to process AR session updates.

With this protocol, the delegate gains access to the following information:

- **Updated Frame Data**: Provides a newly-captured camera image along with AR information to the delegate, provided in an `ARFrame`.

- **Added Anchors**: Informs the delegate that one or more anchors have been added to the session.

- **Removed Anchors**: Informs the delegate that one or more anchors have been removed from the session.

- **Updated Anchors**: Informs the delegate that the session has adjusted the properties of one or more anchors. This is where you can monitor any changes in the blend shapes you're tracking. Modifying a blend shape will trigger a session update.

Adding ARDelegateHandler

For your next step, you'll create a new class that inherits from this protocol so you can track changes to the facial blend shapes.

Add the following class to `ARViewContainer`:

```
// 1
class ARDelegateHandler: NSObject, ARSessionDelegate {
  // 2
  var arViewContainer: ARViewContainer
  // 3
  init(_ control: ARViewContainer) {
    arViewContainer = control
    super.init()
  }
}
```

Here's a closer look at what this does:

1. This defines a new class called `ARDelegateHandler` that inherits `ARSessionDelegate`.
2. When the class instantiates, it provides `ARViewContainer` and stores it in `arViewContainer`.
3. This is the class initializer, which simply stores the provided `ARViewController` then initializes the super class.

From a SwiftUI perspective, you now need to create a custom instance to communicate changes from the view controller to the other parts of the SwiftUI interface. You'll use a `makeCoordinator` to create this custom instance.

To do so, add the following function to `ARViewContainer`:

```
func makeCoordinator() -> ARDelegateHandler {
  ARDelegateHandler(self)
}
```

This defines `makeCoordinator` and indicates that it will provide an instance of `ARDelegateHandler`. It then creates an actual instance of `ARDelegateHandler`, providing `self` as the `ARViewContainer`.

Now that everything's in place, you can set the session delegate for the view. Add the following line of code to `makeUIView(context:)`, just after initializing `arView`:

```
arView.session.delegate = context.coordinator
```

Here, you set the view's session delegate to the context coordinator, which now starts updating the session when it detects any changes.

Handling ARSession updates

With the delegate class in place, you can now start tracking updates to any of the facial blend shapes.

Add the following function to `ARDelegateHandler`:

```
// 1
func session(_ session: ARSession,
  didUpdate anchors: [ARAnchor]) {
  // 2
  guard robot != nil else { return }
  // 3
  var faceAnchor: ARFaceAnchor?
  for anchor in anchors {
    if let a = anchor as? ARFaceAnchor {
      faceAnchor = a
    }
  }
}
```

Here's what's happening above:

1. This defines `session(_:didUpdate:)`, which triggers every time there's an update available on the anchor.

2. You're only interested in anchor updates while the robot scene is active. When `robot` is `nil`, you simply skip any updates.

3. This extracts the first available anchor from the received `anchors` that conforms to an `ARFaceAnchor`, then stores it in `arFaceAnchor`. You'll extract all the updated blend shape information from here.

Tracking blinking eyes

Now that the update handling function is in place, you can inspect the actual blend shape values and use them to update the scene elements so the robot blinks its eyes when the user blinks theirs.

You'll use the **eyeBlinkLeft** and **eyeBlinkRight** blend shapes to track the user's eyes.

Start by adding the following block of code to the bottom of `session(_:didUpdate:)`:

```
let blendShapes = faceAnchor?.blendShapes
let eyeBlinkLeft = blendShapes?[.eyeBlinkLeft]?.floatValue
let eyeBlinkRight = blendShapes?[.eyeBlinkRight]?.floatValue
```

Here, you access the `blendShapes` through the updated `faceAnchor`. You then inspect the specific blend shape key `eyeBlinkLeft` to get its current value, which is provided as a `floatValue`.

Then you use the same approach to get the current value for `eyeBlinkRight`.

Tracking eyebrows

To make the eyes more expressive, you'll use the user's eyebrows to tilt the eyelids inwards or outwards around the z axis. This makes the robot look angry or sad, depending on the user's expression.

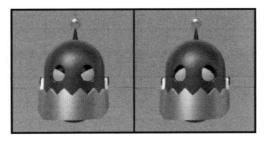

This time, you'll use three blend shapes to track the user's eyebrow movements:

- **browInnerUp**: Tracks the inner, upward movement of both eyebrows.

- **browDownLeft** and **browDownRight**: Tracks the left- and right-side downward movement of the user's eyebrows.

To put them into place, add the following to the bottom of `session(_:didUpdate:)`:

```
let browInnerUp = blendShapes?[.browInnerUp]?.floatValue
let browLeft = blendShapes?[.browDownLeft]?.floatValue
let browRight = blendShapes?[.browDownRight]?.floatValue
```

Great, now you're tracking the eyebrows. The only thing left to do is to align the orientation of the eyelids with these blend shape values. To do it, though, you'll also need to track what the user is doing with their jaw.

Tracking the jaw

Now, you'll track the user's jaw, and use it to update the orientation. You'll use the **jawOpen** blend shape to track the user's jaw movement.

Add the following code to the bottom of `session(_:didUpdate:)`:

```
let jawOpen = blendShapes?[.jawOpen]?.floatValue
```

Now, you're ready to use special vectors to align both the eyelids and the jaw.

Positioning with quaternions

In the next section, you'll update the orientations of the eyelids and jaw based on the blend shape values you're capturing. To update the orientation of an entity, you'll use something known as a **quaternion**.

A **quaternion** is a **four-element vector** used to encode any possible rotation in a 3D coordinate system. A quaternion represents two components: a **rotation axis** and the **amount of rotation** around the rotation axis.

Three vector components, **x**, **y** and **z** represent the axis, while a **w** component represents the rotation amount.

Quaternions are difficult to use. Luckily, there are a few handy functions that make working with them a breeze.

Here are two important quaternion functions you'll use in this chapter:

- **simd_quatf(angle:,axis:)**: Allows you to specify a single rotation by means of an **angle** amount along with the **axis** the rotation will revolve around.

- **simd_mul(p:, q:)**: Lets you multiply two quaternions together to form a single quaternion. Use this function when you want to apply more than one rotation to an entity.

You have to specify angles in **radians**. To make life a little easier, you'll use a little helper function that converts degrees into radians.

Add the following helper function to ARDelegateHandler:

```
func Deg2Rad(_ value: Float) -> Float {
    return value * .pi / 180
}
```

And that's all you need to make the conversion easy.

Updating the eyelids

Now that you've collected all the blend shape data, you need to update the eyelid orientation.

Take a look at a side view of a single eye with an eyelid.

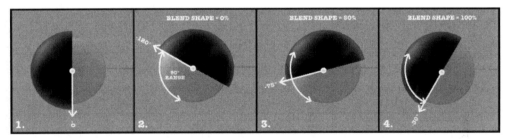

Here's how to use the captured **blink blend shape** data to update the eyelid orientation:

1. Import the eyelid with a rotation around the **x-axis** of **0°**. This is a fully shut eye.

2. To open the eye, set the eyelid's natural resting orientation to **-120°** around the **x-axis**. Then rotate the eyelid through a **90°** ranged angle based on the value of the blink blend shape. When the user's eye is open, the blend shape will be **0%**, adding **0°** to the current resting orientation.

3. As the user closes their eyes, the blink blend shape's value will increase. At a **50%** position, you'll add **45°** to the current resting **-120°** orientation, setting the orientation to about **-75°**. The eyes will appear partially shut now.

4. When the user fully closes their eyes, the blink blend shape increases toward **100%**, adding the full **90°** angle range to the current resting orientation. This makes the eyes appear completely closed.

At the same time, you'll apply a rotation around the **z-axis** to make the eye appear angry or sad. You'll use the same approach with the captured **brow blend shapes**.

Here's what all that looks like in code. Add the following block of code to the bottom of session(_:didUpdate:):

```
// 1
robot.eyeLidL?.orientation = simd_mul(
  // 2
  simd_quatf(
    angle: Deg2Rad(-120 + (90 * eyeBlinkLeft!)),
    axis: [1, 0, 0]),
  // 3
  simd_quatf(
    angle: Deg2Rad((90 * browLeft!) - (30 * browInnerUp!)),
    axis: [0, 0, 1]))
// 4
robot.eyeLidR?.orientation = simd_mul(
  simd_quatf(
    angle: Deg2Rad(-120 + (90 * eyeBlinkRight!)),
    axis: [1, 0, 0]),
  simd_quatf(
    angle: Deg2Rad((-90 * browRight!) - (-30 * browInnerUp!)),
    axis: [0, 0, 1]))
```

This updates both the left and right eyelid orientations:

1. To start, you check the robot is currently the active prop, so you can gain access to elements like the left eyelid via robot. You'll apply two rotations to the orientation of the left eyelid, using quaternion multiplication to combine two quaternions.

2. This is the first rotation around the x-axis. The left eyelid is currently resting at a **-120°** rotation, so you want to use that as the base rotation. You then multiply the left blink blend shape by **90°**, which is the amount of influence the blend shape will have over the eyelid rotation.

3. This is the second rotation around the z-axis. The left brow blend shape has a **90°** influence over the eyelid orientation, while the inner brow movement only has a **30°** influence.

4. You use the same approach to update the right eyelid orientation. The only difference you'll notice is that the eyelid tilts in the opposite direction around the z-axis for the brow movement.

Updating the jaw

The eyelids are done, but you still need to update the jaw orientation with the captured blend shape information:

```
robot.jaw?.orientation = simd_quatf(
  angle: Deg2Rad(-100 + (60 * jawOpen!)),
  axis: [1, 0, 0])
```

Similar to how the eyelids work, the jaw sits at a natural **-100°** with a **60°** range of motion linked to the jaw open blend shape.

And that's it, you're all done! Time for another build and run test.

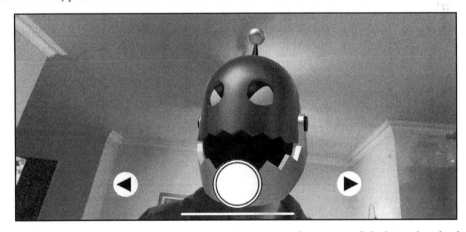

You can now blink, frown and control that huge metal jaw. Careful, this robot looks a bit on the angry side! :]

Adding lasers

The robot is mostly done, but there's always room for improvement. Wouldn't it be cool if it could shoot lasers from its eyes when it gets extra angry?

Well, that's your next task! When the user opens their mouth past a certain point, dangerous lasers will shoot from the robot's eyes.

Here's how you add the lasers. Open **Experience.rcproject** in **Reality Composer**, then select the **Robot** scene.

Add a **Basic ▸ Cylinder** object to the scene.

Select the newly-added cylinder and rename it **Laser_L**. Under the **Transform** section, set the **Position** to **(X:4cm, Y:60cm, Z:-4.5cm)**.

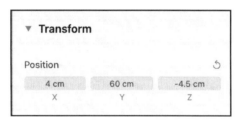

Under the **Look** section, leave the **Material** as **Glossy Paint**, but change the **Material Color** to **Yellow**. Set the **Diameter** to **1 cm**, set the **Height** to **1 m** and set the **Bevel Radius** to **0 cm**.

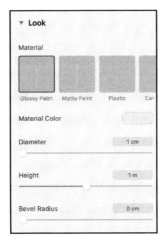

Now, duplicate the cylinder and rename it **Laser_R**. Then under the Transform section, set the **Position** to **(X:-4 cm, Y:60 cm, Z:-4.5 cm)**.

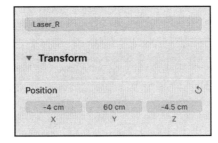

Two lasers should now shoot from the robot's eyes.

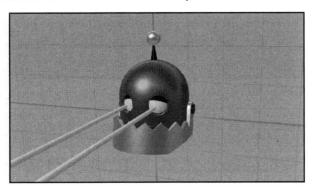

Sending & receiving notifications

Your next goal is to really bring those lasers to life. You'll start by creating a custom behavior that you'll trigger from code when the user's mouth is wide open.

While the lasers are firing, you have to wait for them to finish before you can fire another laser. To achieve that, you'll send a notification to your code to indicate that the laser has finished.

The first thing you need to do is to hide the lasers when the scene starts. Open the **Behaviors** panel, then add a **Start Hidden** behavior.

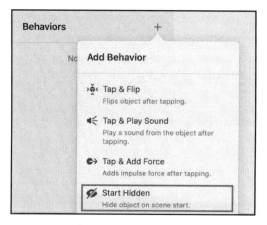

Rename the behavior to **Start** and add the two lasers as the affected objects for the **Hide** action.

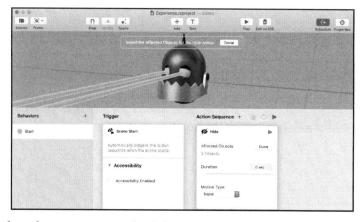

Now, when the robot scene starts, both lasers will be hidden.

With the two lasers selected in the scene, you'll add a **Custom** behavior next.

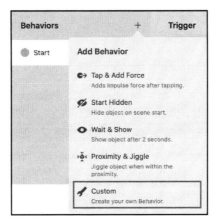

Rename the behavior to **Lasers**, then add the **Trigger** as a **Notification**.

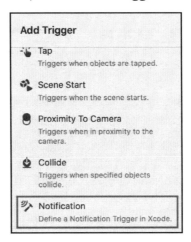

Under the **Notification** trigger, change the **Identifier** to **ShowLasers**.

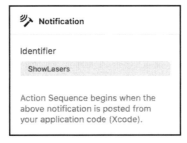

You can now trigger this behavior from code by using the identifier.

Next, you want the lasers to become visible and make a noise, then disappear again.

To make them appear, add a grouped **Show** action with a **Play Sound** action sequence. For the **Show** action, set the **Duration** to **3 sec**. For the **Play Sound** action, set the **Audio Clip** to **DJ Scratching and Effect 23.caf**.

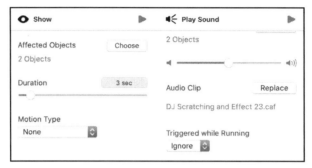

Now, to make them disappear, add a grouped **Hide** action with a **Play Sound** action sequence. For the **Hide** action, set the **Duration** to **3 sec**. For the **Play Sound** action, set the **Audio Clip** to **DJ Scratching and Effect 22.caf**.

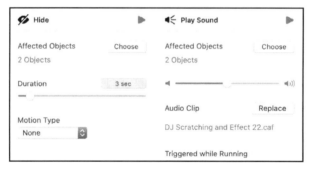

Now, the lasers will appear then disappear over six seconds while making a strange noise.

The last thing you need to do is to create a notification that lets the code know when the action sequence finishes.

With both lasers still selected, under the **Lasers** behavior, add a **Notify** action to the **Action Sequence**.

For the **Notify** action, set the **Identifier** to **LasersDone**.

Now, the Action Sequence can notify the code once the sequence completes.

Save the Reality Composer project, then jump back to Xcode.

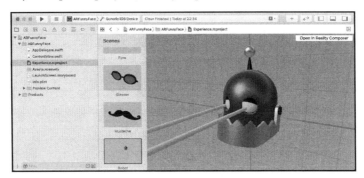

Your changes are now visible in the project. You'll take a look at the coding side of handling notifications next.

Coding the notifications

Now, you'll add the code that prevents other things from happening while the lasers are firing.

Start by adding the following property to the top of the `ARDelegateHandler` class:

```
var isLasersDone = true
```

You'll use this variable to block additional triggers. When this value is `false`, the lasers are currently active and you have to wait for the action sequence to complete before triggering the lasers again.

Add the following block of code to the bottom of `session(_:didUpdate:)`:

```
// 1
if (self.isLasersDone == true && jawOpen! > 0.9) {
  // 2
  self.isLasersDone = false
  // 3
  robot.notifications.showLasers.post()
  // 4
  robot.actions.lasersDone.onAction = { _ in
    self.isLasersDone = true
  }
}
```

Here's its breakdown:

1. If the user's jaw is about **90%** open and the lasers aren't currently active, you can trigger the lasers.

2. Once you trigger the lasers, you need to keep `isLasersDone` set to `false`. That indicates the action sequence is currently active, preventing the user from triggering multiple sequences at the same time.

3. Trigger the custom behavior by finding it under the available `notifications` using the identifier name you defined in behavior.

4. Here, you create an action notification handler that triggers once the action sequence completes. You'll find it under the available `actions` using the identifier name you defined within the notify action. It sets `isLasersDone` back to `true`, letting the user trigger new lasers again.

Congratulations! Build and run now to test the final product.

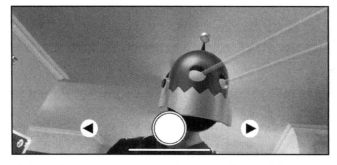

The robot can blink, look sad and angry, and open and close his jaw. But, best of all, it can shoot lasers from its eyes when the user opens their mouth wide. Awesome!

Key points

Congratulations, you've reached the end of this chapter and section. Before grabbing a delicious cup of coffee, quickly take a look at some key points you've learned in this chapter.

To recap:

- **Facial blend shapes**: You've learned about facial blend shapes and how they're used to track a face's key points.
- **ARSessionDelegate**: You learned how to handle scene updates via the `ARSessionDelegate`. Every time a blend shape updates, it triggers a session update, allowing you to update the entities within the scene.
- **Using blend shapes**: You've learned how to track blend shapes and use the data to update entity orientations.
- **Quaternions**: You know what quaternions are and how to use helper functions to demystify them, making rotations a breeze to work with.
- **Notifications**: Triggering actions sequences from code and receiving notify actions from scenes is simple.

Enjoy that cup of coffee. See you in the next section, where you'll learn more about ARKit and SpriteKit.

Section V: ARKit & SpriteKit

In this section, you'll get a full introduction to ARKit and find out what makes it so powerful. In doing so, you'll create a fun 2D SpriteKit game where you get to save tiny Emoji's before they fall to their death.

Chapter 12: ARKit

Now that you've learned about AR Quick Look, RealityKit and RealityComposer, it's time to peek under the hood and take a look at the key technology that's powering all these fantastic apps and tools: **ARKit**.

In this section, you'll combine the power of **ARKit** with the power of **SpriteKit**. You'll create a fun 2D SpriteKit game where you get to pop little emojis before they explode in your face!

In this chapter, you'll focus on ARKit first.

ARKit

> **Note**: This chapter is theory based only. Feel free to jump ahead to the next chapter if you want to get your hands dirty with an ARKit based project.

What is ARKit?

ARKit is Apple's mobile AR development framework. With it, you can create an immersive, engaging experience that allows you to augment virtual 2D and 3D content with the live camera feed of the world around you.

Augmented reality frameworks aren't new. Vuforia, for example, has been around for many years. What sets ARKit apart from other AR frameworks is that ARKit performs **markerless tracking**.

Being markerless means that ARKit doesn't need tracking cards. It understands the world around it and quickly identifies surfaces that it can place virtual content on.

Interestingly enough, older frameworks quickly incorporated ARKit into their APIs, instantly giving them ARKit's awesome markerless tracking capabilities.

ARKit transforms any Apple device with an A9 or higher processor into an AR-capable device. Just think about that for a second: At this very moment, millions of Apple users already have a sophisticated AR-capable device right in their pockets.

> **Note**: As Apple continues to develop new AR-capable hardware for its most recent devices, they improve ARKit, too, to provide support for the newer hardware. It's important to note that some of the more modern ARKit features will only work on devices with specific hardware.

Animojis & Memojis

ARKit is the key technology responsible for making iMessage one of the coolest instant messaging apps out there. ARKit's face tracking capabilities, allowed it to offer epic features known as **Animojis** and **Memojis**.

Using Animojis, you can become a mystical unicorn or a fearless lion. You can record yourself while you puppeteer one of these highly-detailed creatures using your own facial expressions.

Apple's engineers didn't stop there; they simply had to take it even further with **Memojis**.

On the surface, Memojis look like the human counterpart of Animojis, but under the hood lies a very sophisticated character creator engine.

With the power of Memojis, you can re-create and transform yourself into a fun animated character. You can then turn on the selfie camera and allow the magic of ARKit to bring yourself to life.

Even apps like FaceTime have started incorporating Memojis. You now have even more freedom of choice to express yourself while meeting with friends, family and colleagues.

I personally love to use it, especially on those bad hair days… which is every day, nowadays.

Early 2020   Late 2020

Handsome as always, but wow, do I need a haircut! :]

Technologies behind ARKit

You might be surprised to find that some of the technologies behind ARKit are quite familiar and have been around for a while.

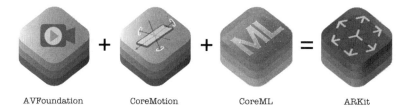

AVFoundation   CoreMotion   CoreML   ARKit

- **AVFoundation**: ARKit uses this framework to gain full control over audio and video input and output.

- **CoreMotion**: ARKit uses **Visual Inertial Odometry** (VIO) to track the motion of the device and the world around it. VIO fuses the AVFoundation-based input from the camera sensor with the device motion data captured via CoreMotion.

- **CoreML**: ARKit uses **machine learning** to speed up surface detection and surface classification. It's also the key technology behind ARKit's object and image recognition and processing, as well as face and body detection.

If you've used any of these frameworks before, it's easy to recognize how they work together to support ARKit's advanced recognition and tracking capabilities.

Rendering integration with ARKit

Interestingly enough, ARKit doesn't have its own graphics API; it only provides world-space-tracking and scene-understanding capabilities. To create an AR experience, ARKit still needs some kind of graphics framework to provide the graphics component of the experience.

Fortunately, ARKit provides easy integration for familiar graphics frameworks and popular game engines, including:

SpriteKit   SceneKit   RealityKit   Metal   Unity   Unreal

- **SpriteKit**: A high-level 2D graphics framework for drawing shapes, particle effects, text, animated sprites and video. It has its own built-in physics engine and is built on top of Metal to achieve the best possible performance.

- **SceneKit**: A high-level 3D graphics framework for creating 3D scenes and special effects with geometry, materials, lights, particle systems and cameras. It, too, has its own built-in physics engine and is built on top of Metal for the best possible performance.

- **RealityKit**: A high-level 3D graphics framework built from the ground up on top of Metal specifically for AR. It offers geometry, materials and lights along with its own built-in physics engine.

- **Metal**: Apple's lowest-level graphics API, providing developers the fastest and most direct access to the Graphics Processing Unit.

- **Unity & Unreal**: Apple's relationships with the gaming development community have resulted in some excellent plug-ins for popular game engines like **Unity** and **Unreal**.

ARKit makes it easy to integrate with graphics frameworks such as SpriteKit, SceneKit, RealityKit and Metal.

ARKit-powered app examples

To demonstrate ARKit's capabilities, here are some examples of interesting ARKit-powered apps you can find for free on the Apple AppStore. Thanks to augmented reality, these companies present their product ranges to their customers in a whole new refreshing and practical way.

IKEA Place

IKEA Place is a digital catalog of lifelike, true-to-scale 3D furniture. Thanks to the power of ARKit, customers can preview IKEA's furniture in their own homes, giving them a real sense of the furniture's scale and ascetics.

Find it on the AppStore here: https://apple.co/31Zjoot

Warby Parker

Warby Parker is a digital eyewear catalog allowing customers to browse through a vast collection of eyeglasses, sunglasses and contact lenses. With ARKit's face detection and tracking capabilities, customers can virtually try out and preview frames.

Find it on the AppStore here: https://apple.co/3fiHUVq

Minecraft Earth

Get to experience Minecraft in a whole new way with **Minecraft Earth**. With ARKit's help, players can now enjoy this classic game in augmented reality. They can build amazing creations in tabletop mode or in life-size mode, and even collaborate and build together.

ARKit's features

If you have prior experience with Apple's other frameworks, you might expect ARKit to have a long and painful learning curve.

Fear not, because ARKit's actually quite simple — it only takes a few lines of code to get things working. ARKit does most of the heavy lifting for you so you can focus on what's important: Creating an immersive and engaging AR experience.

So what can ARKit do for you? Take a look and prepare to be blown away.

World space tracking

ARKit tracks the device's position and orientation in real time through real-world space.

It uses sampled motion data from the device to automatically update the virtual content transforms. It then uses the captured motion data to move a virtual camera through a virtual scene.

This mimics the actual real-world position and orientation of the device in the virtual scene.

Scene understanding & persistence

To achieve markerless tracking, ARKit creates and manages its own map of the surfaces and feature points it detects, then stores that map in a point cloud. Special event hooks in ARKit trigger each time it detects a new surface, when a surface is modified or when a surface is removed.

This gives you incredible control over your scene, including how your content interacts with these surfaces.

ARKit can also load and save world maps for quick recognition of previously-scanned spaces. With the same world map loaded on multiple devices, you can easily create a shared experience with a basic network.

You can also keep virtual content persistent across multiple ARKit sessions. How about playing hide and seek with yourself, trying to find where you left your virtual coffee mug?! :]

Light estimation

ARKit can provide accurate real-world lighting conditions. It analyzes the active video feed frame data to calculate the estimated environmental lighting conditions, and then provides a light source to light your virtual scene.

If your virtual content uses physically-based materials, your content will blend into the real-world environment more realistically. This feature means that when you turn the lights off in your room, your virtual 3D content will dim, too.

Real-time environment map

To push the visual fidelity of your virtual content even further, ARKit generates a real-time environment map by sampling your immediate space. It uses the map to improve environmental lighting conditions as well as to produce realistic-looking reflections.

For example, when you place a shiny virtual bowl next to a juicy real-world apple lying on a table, you'll see the apple's reflection on the bowl.

Scene interaction

For unrestricted interaction with the 3D content within your AR scenes, use ARKit's provided hit-test functions.

You can also couple interaction with traditional touch-based gestures, which Apple recommends in its Human Interface Guidelines, specifically for AR-based apps.

However, because you're inside Apple's ecosystem, nothing's stopping you from using any of Apple's other great frameworks like CoreML or Vision. You can even use SiriKit and command the AR experience with your voice.

Metric scaling system

To calculate distances and sizes in your scene, ARKit uses an accurate metric scaling system. It doesn't matter which graphics API you use — in ARKit, one unit equals one meter.

This allows you to create 3D models that appear accurately scaled when you place them into the real-world.

Now, you can test if that big couch you always wanted will fit into the living room.

2D image detection & tracking

ARKit can detect and track up to 100 images and rectangular shapes at a time. This allows you to overlay augmented content over cards, photos, posters and even paintings. ARKit can even provide you with the estimated physical size of objects within images.

Bringing static images and paintings to life has never been easier. How about giving the Mona Lisa a grin?

3D object detection

Create your very own AR recognition models of physical 3D objects. Once you give it an AR model, ARKit can detect that physical 3D object, even in fairly complex environments. How about blowing some smoke out of a toy car exhaust?

Face detection & tracking

ARKit can do face detection and tracking on devices equipped with an A12 Bionic chip and later, which powers front-facing camera experiences. Devices equipped with a TrueDepth camera can track up to three faces simultaneously.

With this, you can create your own Animoji characters and have some fun with friends and family.

Multi-camera tracking

You can simultaneously use face and world tracking on the front and back cameras, opening up new possibilities.

Now you can puppeteer a virtual dancing character while controlling its facial movements with your own facial expressions.

Motion capture

Real-time motion capture allows you to track a person's body position, movement and pose and produces a 3D skeleton consisting of joints and bones.

You can use this information as input into your own AR experiences, or you can store the captured information to animate your own game characters.

People occlusion

AR experiences are now much more immersive, thanks to people occlusion. This is a green-screen-style effect made possible by machine learning.

ARKit can let your AR content pass in front and behind of real-world human figures by using depth-based occlusion. This effect is vastly better on newer devices equipped with a LiDAR scanner.

Depth API

ARKit provides a **Depth API** for devices equipped with a LiDAR scanner. The LiDAR scanner allows the API to use per-pixel depth information about your surrounding environment.

Combining advanced scene understanding capabilities with 3D mesh data pushes them to the next level. This improves virtual object occlusion and placement, making objects blend into the physical surroundings much more realistically.

Scene geometry

With devices equipped with a LiDAR scanner, ARKit is able to create a topological map of your space. Thanks to machine learning, ARKit has a deep understanding of your environment, too. It can place labels next to identified content like floors, walls, ceilings, windows, doors and even seats. It can then use all this information to provide object occlusion and real-world physics for your virtual content.

Geo location anchors

ARKit allows you to place AR content based on geolocation. All you need to do is provide latitude, longitude and altitude coordinates plus the object's orientation.

Now, you can place AR content anywhere in the world for users to experience. Anybody up for catching some Pokémon?

Instant AR

LiDAR-equipped devices are capable of incredibly fast plane detection, which allows ARKit to instantly place AR content into the real world without even having to scan the space.

Collaborative sessions

Create shared AR experiences with live collaborative sessions between multiple users. ARKit builds a collaborative world map between multiple users, allowing them to get into a shared AR experience much faster — and, ultimately, making the development of shared AR experiences easier and faster, too.

ARKit's limitations

ARKit presents a new paradigm for user experiences on mobile devices. It does, however, have some limiting qualities that impact the user's AR experience. As a developer, you should be aware of these limitations.

Surface detection takes time

If your user is using a device without a LiDAR scanner, surface detection and real-world understanding take a noticeable amount of time.

Sure, surface detection has come a long way since it was initially introduced. However, it's still important to manage user expectations and guide them through the surface detection stage of your app.

To help with this, ARKit offers a standardized AR onboarding process that you can use.

Motion processing lag

With AR experiences, you'll quickly notice that excessive device motion can cause stuttering and blurred imaging, which makes it difficult for ARKit to understand what it's looking at. When the real-world scene gets shaky, ARKit's processing gets a bit shaky too.

It's important to notify the user of these issues. ARKit does provide you with various events that you can use to detect these issues and handle them proactively.

Low-light conditions

Low-light conditions are problematic. The on-device camera cannot discern low-light scenes as well as the human eye can, which means ARKit has trouble with scene detection when the lights are dim. It may even fail to recognize any surfaces at all.

As a rule of thumb, if it's night bright enough for you to see clearly, ARKit is struggling even more.

Smooth & reflective surfaces

ARKit has difficulty detecting and tracking smooth, textureless and even reflective surfaces. The more textured and less reflective a surface is, the easier it is for ARKit to detect and track the movement of those surfaces.

As a developer, your job is to make sure your users understand these kinds of limitations before using your AR-enabled app. Otherwise, they'll get frustrated when they can't place virtual furniture onto shiny, polished, jet-black marble floors.

Ghost effect

After using AR for a while, you might notice some virtual content disobeys the laws of physics. For example, the virtual content might pass through real-world objects, much like a ghost would pass through a closed door.

Since situations like this can break the AR experience, it's a good idea to encourage users to use your app in wide-open spaces or on top of a nice, clean table.

Apple is hard at work to improve the overall experience with the introduction of people and object occlusion. Who knows, perhaps Apple is already working on how to occlude those pesky pets that are always getting in the way? :]

Hardware limitations

As a developer, you have to be aware that some ARKit features are only available on certain Apple devices.

ARKit provides ways to check for feature availability. Make sure your app uses these methods to ensure that your app is stable and that the user has the optimum immersive AR experience.

ARKit resources

Apple provides a large collection of important resources in the form of documentation, videos and sample apps for you to learn from. Finding these resources can be challenging, so here's a curated list for you:

Official ARKit documentation

This is Apple's official site for ARKit documentation. Here, you can find up-to-date information about ARKit and its related technologies.

- **Apple Developer Documentation for ARKit**: http://apple.co/2sE0rUq

Human Interface Guidelines for augmented reality

Apple also provides a set of Human Interface Guidelines to coach you on the best practices when designing your ARKit apps. This guide shows you exactly what to do — and what not to do. Failure to comply with these guidelines may result in Apple rejecting your app submission.

- **Human Interface Guidelines for AR**: http://apple.co/2xOwp1Q

Official WWDC videos on ARKit

Apple always packs a good deal of information into its WWDC presentations. Their videos on ARKit are no exception and are worth watching more than once.

- **ARKit video's from WWDC 2017 to 2020**: https://apple.co/2NxL2TX

Interactive content with ARKit

This is one of Apple's official ARKit demos, and it's a fun way to get some hands-on experience with ARKit.

Follow the link and look for the **Download Sample Code** button. Once you find it, download the .zip file, extract the contents and build the project using the latest version of Xcode.

You'll need to run it on a physical device with an A9 processor or better (iPhone SE, iPhone 6s and later models). At this time, you can't test AR apps on the simulator.

In this demo, you'll get to meet Elon the chameleon, but be careful — he's always watching!

- **Interactive Content with ARKit:** http://apple.co/2yI4gi2

Key points

You've reached the end of the chapter, but your journey of creating AR-enabled games and apps with ARKit has just begun.

Here's a quick recap of some of the most important things you've learned about ARKit in this chapter:

- **ARKit**: You now know what ARKit is and the power it can add to your games and apps.
- **Surface detection & tracking**: ARKit makes it easy to detect viable real-world surfaces where you can place your AR content.
- **Scene Understanding**: Not only can ARKit track various types of surfaces, but with the power of machine learning, it's also capable of understanding what it's seeing and can even tell you what the types of surfaces are.
- **Image detection & tracking**: Detecting and tracking posters, paintings or even business cards is a breeze with ARKit.
- **Object detection**: ARKit can Detect and augment real-world objects.
- **Face detection & tracking**: ARKit's the key technology behind features like Animojis and Memojis. You can harness the power of ARKit to create your own augmented face experiences.
- **Occlusion**: ARKit's ability to occlude people and objects is slowly by surely improving. With capable devices, basic occlusion is standard, which has the power to make occlusion-related issues a thing of the past.
- **Graphics Frameworks**: ARKit isn't a graphics library; instead it's a framework that does the heavy lifting of AR for you. It offers easy integration for graphics frameworks and there are also plugins available for popular game engines.

In the next chapter, you'll learn how to create your first ARKit app powered by SpriteKit using Xcode. See you soon!

Chapter 13: ARKit & SpriteKit

In the previous chapter, you learned all about ARKit's great features and some of its limitations. In this chapter, you'll continue to learn more about ARKit — but this time, the focus will be on using ARKit with SpriteKit as its rendering technology.

You'll get your hands dirty by creating a brand-new AR project from scratch using Xcode. You'll create a fun AR experience that uses 2D-based emoji graphics. Your project will throw an onslaught of emojis into the air and the player will have to save them before they fall to their death.

Keen on seeing emojis fall to their death? Then what are you waiting for? Jump in and get those hands dirty!

What is SpriteKit?

SpriteKit is Apple's general-purpose 2D graphics framework. You can use it to draw shapes, particles, text, sprites and video.

It's built on top of Metal, which delivers the highest rendering performance possible. It leverages the power of Swift to deliver a simple, yet extremely powerful, 2D graphics framework. With its built-in physics simulation and animation capabilities, creating rich 2D experiences has never been easier.

Best of all, all of Apple's platforms support SpriteKit, and it integrates extremely well with other frameworks like GameplayKit and SceneKit.

So start Xcode, it's time to create the project.

Creating a SpriteKit AR project

Create a new project in Xcode. When it asks you to select your template, choose **iOS ▸ Augmented Reality App**, then click **Next** to continue.

Change the **Product Name** to **EmojiPop** and choose **SpriteKit** for the **Content Technology**. You'll use a **Storyboard** UI, so leave the **Interface** as-is and leave the **Language** as **Swift**.

Turn off **Include Tests**, then click **Next** to continue:

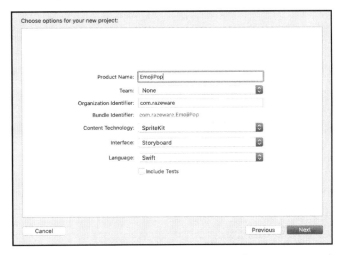

Choose a secure location to save your project. The **Desktop** is a great location for quick projects. You don't need to create a Git repository, so turn that off for now and click **Create** to complete the process.

Xcode will now generate a bare-bones SpriteKit-based Augmented Reality project for you. Once it's done, you'll have a fully-functional project that looks like this:

Before doing anything else, take the project for a quick spin. Connect your device and do a quick build and run to deploy it.

Take the project for a walk in your garden. Tap the screen to spawn lots of little Space Invaders all over. Nice!

A few things to note:

- **Position**: When you tap the screen, a critter spawns into existence based on the position of your device in real-world space.

- **Orientation**: Did you notice how the little critter keeps looking at you, even when you move? Don't freak out, this is just a cool feature known as **billboarding**, which makes 2D sprites always face the camera in 3D space. That way, you'll never see the flat side of the image.

- **Anchors**: Once they spawn into the world, the little critters maintain their position in real-world space, no matter where you move. This is due to **anchoring**, which connects the virtual object to the real world, keeping the anchor at a constant position.

- **Debug Info**: At the bottom-right of the screen, you'll see some debug information. In this instance, you see how many critters have spawned in the form of nodes. You can also see the current frame rate, running at a smooth 60 frames per second.

OK, enough fresh air, go back to your workspace and take a look at what's inside the project.

Exploring the project

In Xcode, with the project open, explore the important components that Xcode generated for you based on the **SpriteKit Augmented Reality Template** project.

AppDelegate.swift

This is the standard starting point of your app.

LaunchScreen.storyboard

The launch screen is another standard part of every app. It's the first thing the user sees when they launch your app.

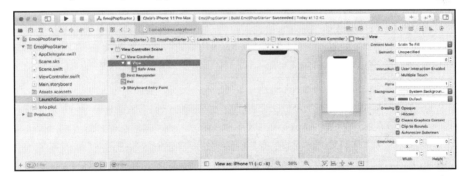

This is where you'll place a beautiful splash image that represents your app.

Main.storyboard

The main storyboard is the view component of your AR app, containing the app's UI. This is a good place to put buttons and heads-up displays, for example.

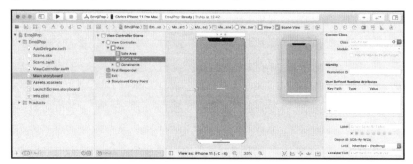

Take particular note of the `ARSKView` scene view class, which lets you overlay an AR scene over a live background image feed from the camera. It provides seamless integration between ARKit and SpriteKit. Also, note that the view is connected to an `@IBOutlet` defined in **ViewController.swift**.

ViewController.swift

The view controller contains the code behind the entire AR experience, specifically for the main storyboard.

Take note of the frameworks at play:

- **UIKit**: This framework provides the required infrastructure for iOS and tvOS apps including the window and view architecture to implement the UI, event handling and input. It also provides support for animation, document, drawing, printing, device information, text and display, search, accessibility, app extension and resource management.

- **SpriteKit**: The framework for 2D graphic support.

- **ARKit**: The framework for AR support.

The `ViewController` inherits directly from the standard `UIViewController`, which provides the infrastructure for managing the views of a basic UIKit-based app.

It also adopts the `ARSKViewDelegate` protocol from ARKit, which contains methods you can implement to synchronize your SpriteKit content with your AR session.

Take special note of `@IBOutlet`. It connects to `ARSKView`, which is defined in the **Main.storyboard**.

Look at `viewDidLoad()` and you'll see that it enables the `showFPS` and `showNodeCount` debug information for the scene view. This is also where the app loads and presents the default `SKScene` scene named **Scene**.

`viewWillAppear(_:)` is where an `ARWorldTrackingConfiguration` instance is created. This configuration is provided to the view's `ARSession` when the user starts it.

Scene.sks

This defines an empty SpriteKit scene.

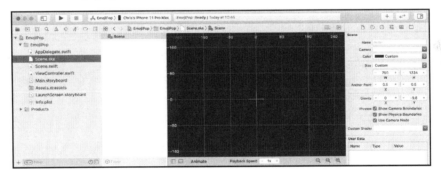

This is the scene that's loaded and presented in the view controller.

Scene.swift

This contains the code behind the SpriteKit scene.

It defines a Scene class that inherits from SKScene. It provides overrides like didMove(to:), which is called when the scene is presented, and update(_:), which is called once every frame. As always, this is where you can handle touch input too.

Assets.xcassets

Here, you'll find your stock-standard app assets like your app icon, for example.

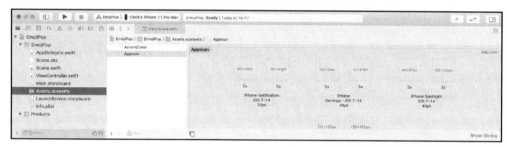

> **Note:** There are a bunch of icons in **starter/resources/AppIcon**. Feel free to drag and drop them here to give your game a cool-looking icon.

Info.plist

When your app runs for the first time, it has to ask for permission to access the camera. ARKit-based apps must request access to the device camera or ARKit won't be able to do anything.

Privacy - Camera Usage Description is the message the user will see when your app requests access to the camera upon start. Feel free to change the description to something more human-readable, like: **AR experience requires access to camera**.

ARSKView & ARSession

The `ARSKView` **(Augmented Reality SpriteKit View)** is a special class used to create 2D SpiteKit AR experiences. It allows you to place 2D content into 3D space within the camera view.

The view includes an `ARSession` object, which is responsible for ARKit's motion tracking and image processing. It's session-based, which means you have to create an AR session instance then **run** it to start the AR tracking process.

Creating a heads-up display (HUD)

For this particular AR experience, you'll need a basic **Heads-Up Display (HUD)** to show the player important information.

> **Note**: To save time building the UI, you'll take a few shortcuts to keep things short and simple, but still functional.

Open **Main.storyboard** and get ready to add a HUD to it. In this instance, the HUD will just be a **Label**.

Open the **Object Library** and search for a `UILabel`. Drag and drop it onto the `ARView` in the design space, snapping it nicely at the center of the top of the screen.

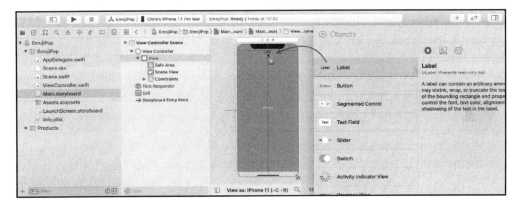

Adjust the label size so it fits across the width of the screen and set the height to 40 units.

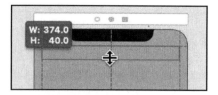

Add some **Constraints** to keep the label at the top and stretched across the screen. Constrain the label to the **top**, **left**, **right** and **height**. Finally, select **Add 4 Constraints** to apply the constraints so the label is fully responsive.

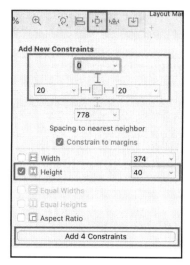

Under the **Attributes Inspector**, clear the **Text** value. Change the **Color** to **White** and set the **Font** to **System Bold 21.0**. Lastly, set the **Alignment** to **Centered**.

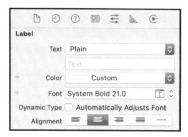

Rename the label to **HUD**, then open a side-by-side view. Select **ViewController.swift** so it's open at the side.

Hold down the **Control** key then, from the storyboard side, click and drag a connection from the **HUD** label into **ViewController.swift** to insert an **outlet**.

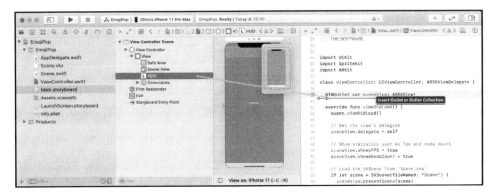

Name the outlet **hudLabel** and select **Connect** to create the `@IBOutlet`..

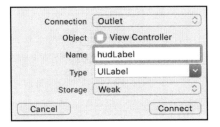

Great, now you can access the label that you'll use as the HUD.

Updating the HUD

With the HUD in place, you need a way to update the displayed message while the game is running.

Open **Scene.swift** and add the following helper function to bottom of Scene:

```
func updateHUD(_ message: String) {
  guard let sceneView = self.view as? ARSKView else {
    return
  }
  let viewController = sceneView.delegate as! ViewController
  viewController.hudLabel.text = message
}
```

With this function in place, you'll be able to update the message displayed in the HUD. Now, you can provide valuable instructions to the player.

Adding game state

A good way to control the game is to add some kind of game state management. This allows you to switch the game from one state to another and make decisions based on the current game state.

Open **Scene.swift** and add the following enum to the top of it, just after the `imports` section:

```
public enum GameState {
   case Init
   case TapToStart
   case Playing
   case GameOver
}
```

Your game will use the following states:

- **Init**: While in this state, the key components of the game are still being initialized. Once everything is ready to go, the game moves into a **TapToStart** state.

- **TapToStart**: While in this state, the HUD will display the message **TAP TO START**, which is an instruction to the player to tap the screen to start the game. Once the player taps the screen, the app creates an AR anchor and places a little box in view of the player. The box acts as a visual indicator that shows the emojis' spawn point to the player. The game starts and moves into the **Playing** state.

- **Playing**: While in this state, emojis will spawn into existence from the box at the spawn point. The player has to catch each emoji before it falls to its death. During this time, the HUD displays the player's current score and total lives left. Once all lives are lost, the game moves into a **GameOver** state.

- **GameOver**: While in the this state, the HUD displays **Game Over** along with the player's final score. The player can tap again to continue, which will move the game back into the **TapToStart** state.

Declaring game variables

Other than the game state, you'll use a few other variables to control important aspects of your game.

Declare the following variables at the top of Scene:

```
var gameState = GameState.Init
var anchor: ARAnchor?
var emojis = "😀😃😄😁😆😅😂🤣😊😇🤴💀👽"
var spawnTime : TimeInterval = 0
var score : Int = 0
var lives : Int = 10
```

This code declares six new properties. Here's what each one does:

- **gameSate**: This maintains the current game state. You'll use it to control the game.

- **anchor**: This contains the only AR anchor for the game. When the player starts the game, it creates a single anchor. This acts as the location in the real world where the emojis will spawn.

- **emojis**: This is a string filled with a bunch of fun emojis. The game will randomly spawn any one of these emojis while the user is playing.

- **spawnTime**: This timed interval controls the rate of spawn. The app uses this to spawn an emoji every 0.5 seconds.

- **score**: This stores the player's current score, incrementing every time the player saves an emoji.

- **lives**: When the player misses an emoji, the emoji falls to its death and the player loses a life. This variable keeps track of the player's available lives. Once this number reaches 0, the game ends.

Add the following game state management functions to the bottom of Scene:

```
public func startGame() {
  gameState = .TapToStart
  updateHUD("- TAP TO START -")
}

public func playGame() {
  gameState = .Playing
  score = 0
  lives = 10
```

```
    spawnTime = 0
}

public func stopGame() {
    gameState = .GameOver
    updateHUD("GAME OVER! SCORE: " + String(score))
}
```

Now you can control the current state of the game by calling these different functions. Take a look at them in detail:

- **startGame()**: Places the game into the **TapToStart** state and displays the message: **TAP TO START**.

- **playGame()**: Places the game into the **Play** state and resets the **score**, **lives** and **spawnTime**.

- **stopGame()**: Places the game into the **GameOver** state and displays the message: **GAME OVER! SCORE:** followed by the actual score for the last game played.

Replace the existing contents of `touchesBegan(_:with:)` with the following `switch` statement:

```
switch (gameState)
{
  case .Init:
    break

  case .TapToStart:
    playGame()
    break

  case .Playing:
    //checkTouches(touches)
    break

  case .GameOver:
    startGame()
    break
}
```

The way you track touches in your game will vary depending on the game's current state. The switch controls the flow of touch events based on the current game state.

- **Init**: While in this state, the app ignores all touch input.
- **TapToStart**: Here, the app is waiting for touch input. When the player touches the screen, the app starts the game.
- **Playing**: In this state, the app checks if the player touched a spawned emoji. If they did, the app will remove that emoji.
- **GameOver**: Once in this mode, the game is over. When the player taps the screen, the app restarts the game.

> **Note**: The call to checkTouches() is currently commented out because that function doesn't exist yet. You'll add it a little later.

Creating a spawn point

With all that in place, it's time to start the game. When the app starts, the view controller will load **Scene.sks**. Once loaded, the app presents the scene to the user and calls didMove(to:). This is a great place to start the game.

With **Scene.swift** still open, add a call to startGame() in didMove(to:):

```
startGame()
```

The game is placed in **TapToStart** state and the player receives the instruction to tap the screen to start the game.

Now, when the player does tap the screen, the app has to create an anchor along with a spawn point.

Add the following function to the bottom of Scene:

```
func addAnchor() {
  // 1
  guard let sceneView = self.view as? ARSKView else {
    return
  }
  // 2
  if let currentFrame = sceneView.session.currentFrame {
    // 3
```

```
        var translation = matrix_identity_float4x4
        translation.columns.3.z = -0.5
        let transform = simd_mul(currentFrame.camera.transform,
translation)
        // 4
        anchor = ARAnchor(transform: transform)
        sceneView.session.add(anchor: anchor!)
    }
}
```

Take a closer look at what's happening here:

1. This casts the `view` as an `SKSView` so you can access the current AR session.

2. This gets the current active frame from the AR session, which contains the camera. You'll use the cameras transform information to create an AR anchor in front of the camera view.

3. This calculates a new transform located 50cm in front of the camera's view.

4. Finally, this creates an AR anchor with the new transform information and adds it to the AR session.

Now, to call to this function, add the following to the bottom of `playGame()`:

```
addAnchor()
```

When the player taps the screen, the game will change state and add an AR anchor 50cm in front of the player.

Now, for the reverse. When the game restarts, you need to remove the previously-added anchor.

To do this, add the following function to the bottom of `Scene`:

```
func removeAnchor() {
    guard let sceneView = self.view as? ARSKView else {
        return
    }
    if anchor != nil {
        sceneView.session.remove(anchor: anchor!)
    }
}
```

This checks whether there's already an active anchor. If there is, it removes the anchor from the AR session.

Now, add a call to `removeAnchor()` at the bottom of `startGame()`:

```
removeAnchor()
```

Excellent! When the game restarts now, the app removes any existing anchors along with all the SpriteKit nodes associated with it.

ARSKViewDelegate

If you recall, the `ViewController` adopted the `ARSKViewDelegate` protocol. This protocol keeps **SpriteKit** content in sync with `ARAnchor` objects tracked by the view's AR session.

It offers the following functions that you can use:

- **func view(_:nodeFor:) -> SKNode**: Call this when the app adds a new AR anchor. Note that it returns a `SKNode`, so this is a good place to create and link a SpriteKit node to the newly-added AR anchor.

- **func view(_:didAdd:for:)**: Informs the delegate that a SpriteKit node related to a new AR anchor has been added to the scene.

- **func view(_:willUpdate:for:)**: Informs the delegate that a SpriteKit node will be updated based on changes to the related AR anchor.

- **func view(_:didUpdate:for:)**: Informs the delegate that a SpriteKit node has been updated to match changes on the related AR anchor.

- **func view(_:didRemove:for:)**: Informs the delegate that the SpriteKit node has been removed from the scene on the related AR anchor.

Adding a spawn point

After the app creates the AR anchor, you'll use the delegate to provide a `SKNode` for the new anchor. This SpriteKit node acts as the **Spawn Point** for the game.

Open **ViewController.swift**, then find `view(_:nodeFor:) -> SKNode` and replace its contents with the following:

```
// 1
let spawnNode = SKNode()
spawnNode.name = "SpawnPoint"
```

```
// 2
let boxNode = SKLabelNode(text: "🆘")
boxNode.verticalAlignmentMode = .center
boxNode.horizontalAlignmentMode = .center
boxNode.zPosition = 100
boxNode.setScale(1.5)
spawnNode.addChild(boxNode)
// 3
return spawnNode
```

Take a look at the code:

1. This creates an empty SpriteKit node and sets its name to **SpawnPoint**.

2. To give the player a visual indicator of where the spawn point is in the real world, this creates a little SOS box and adds it as a child of the spawn point node.

3. Finally, the spawnNode is provided as the SKNode for the newly-added AR anchor. This also links the spawn node to the AR anchor. Any changes to the AR anchor will be synced to the spawn node.

Do a quick build and run to test how it works.

The game starts and the HUD shows **TAP TO START**. When the player taps the screen, a small SOS box spawns into view, anchored to that location.

This might not look like much, but you're making great progress. You've gotten all the ground work out of the way.

Handling problems with the AR session

Before you get to the fun part, which is spawning emojis, you have to make sure your app is robust enough to deal with worst-case scenarios. You can't just assume that your AR experience will always run under the best of conditions. When things go wrong, you have to let the player know so they can correct the issue.

AR issues come in the following forms:

- **AR Session Failures**: Typically occur when the AR session has stopped due to some kind of failure.

- **AR Camera Tracking Issues**: These occur when the quality of ARKit's position tracking has degraded for some reason.

- **AR Session Interruptions**: This issue happens when the session has temporarily stopped processing frames and device position tracking — typically because the player took a phone call or switched to a different app.

You'll use an alert message to notify the player of any issues.

With **ViewControll.swift** open, add the following helper function to the bottom of `ViewController`:

```swift
func showAlert(_ title: String, _ message: String) {
  let alert = UIAlertController(title: title, message: message,
    preferredStyle: .alert)
  alert.addAction(UIAlertAction(title: "OK",
    style: UIAlertAction.Style.default, handler: nil))
  self.present(alert, animated: true, completion: nil)
}
```

This defines a function named `showAlert(_:_:)`, which creates and presents a basic alert with the provided title and message. You also add an **OK** action button so the player can dismiss the alert.

Handling AR session failures

The only thing you really can do when an AR session fails is to inform the player of the issue.

Add the following line of code to `session(_:didFailWithError:)`:

```swift
showAlert("Session Failure", error.localizedDescription)
```

When the session fails, the player will see an alert message with the detailed information from the provided error message in `error.localizedDescription`.

Handling camera tracking issues

When the AR tracking conditions degrade, you can check a few things to try to determine what the problem is. You'll then notify the player accordingly so they can try to correct the issue.

Add the following function to `ViewController`:

```
func session(_ session: ARSession,
  cameraDidChangeTrackingState camera: ARCamera) {
// 1
switch camera.trackingState {
  case .normal: break
  case .notAvailable:
    showAlert("Tracking Limited", "AR not available")
    break
// 2
  case .limited(let reason):
    switch reason {
    case .initializing, .relocalizing: break
    case .excessiveMotion:
      showAlert("Tracking Limited", "Excessive motion!")
      break
    case .insufficientFeatures:
      showAlert("Tracking Limited", "Insufficient features!")
      break
    default: break
    }
  }
}
```

When the camera changes tracking state, the app notifies this delegate function. You then need to interrogate the provided tracking state for more information.

Take a look at what exactly it's doing:

1. You can access the current tracking state through the provided camera. Th `switch` statement then handles all possible cases. If there's a problem, you then notify the player with an alert message.

2. When tracking is **limited**, you can dig deeper to find out exactly why. Again, you have a few cases to deal with. You'll then send the player an alert message with the result.

Handling AR session interruptions

If something like a phone call or switching to another app interrupts the AR session, there's a good chance you'll have to restart everything. Luckily, there are delegates that help you handle this.

Add the following to `sessiongWasInterrupted(_:)`:

```
showAlert("AR Session", "Session was interrupted!")
```

When the player returns to the game, this simply notifies the player that there was an interruption to the game so it stopped.

Add the following to `sessionInterruptedEnded(_:)`:

```
let scene = sceneView.scene as! Scene
scene.startGame()
```

This makes sure your game restarts properly, by moving the game into a **TAP TO START** state. It also removes all the SpriteKit nodes and the spawn point anchor.

Do a final build and run to test all the changes. You can test a few things now:

- **Session Interruption**: Start the game, switch over to another app, then return to the game. You'll get an alert message stating **Session was Interrupted** and the game will return to the **TAP TO START** state.

- **Limited Camera Tracking**: Stick your finger over the camera lens so the scene goes dark. This forces a limited tracking issue, and you'll receive an alert message with the exact reason why.

Key points

Fantastic, you've reached the end of this chapter. You can find a copy of the project in its current state under **final/EmojiPop**.

Here's a quick recap of what you've learned:

- **ARKit & SpriteKit**: You've learned how easy it is to create an ARKit-based project that uses SpriteKit as the key content technology. You also got an in-depth overview of the project content that the AR project template generated for you.

- **ARSKView & ARSession**: You now know about the AR view that's responsible for rendering augmented SpriteKit content. You also know about the AR session that's responsible for ARKit's motion tracking and image processing.

- **HUD**: You learned how to create a basic heads-up display using the standard storyboard with a label. This is a simple way to give the player important alerts and updates.

- **Game State Management**: You implemented basic game state management, which allows you to keep things under control based on the current state of the game.

- **ARAnchor & ARSKViewDelegate**: You learned how to add an anchor to an AR session and how to keep your SpriteKit content synchronized by using `ARSKViewDelegate` to track when an anchor is added, updated or removed.

- **AR Session Issues**: Elegantly handling possible AR session-related issues is vital makes your AR apps robust, delivering a high-quality AR experience for the player.

Go grab yourself a well deserved break, but don't stay away too long. In the next chapter, you'll finally get to spawn those emojis — and you'll get to move them with physics!

Chapter 14: Raycasting & Physics

In this chapter, you'll pick up from where you left off in the previous one. Your AR-based SpriteKit game is coming along well, and you've laid a lot of the groundwork already. Your goal now is to add all the missing pieces and finishing touches.

Take a moment to take stock of what you've done and what's up next.

What's done?

- **Game State**: The game has basic game states in place, and you can easily switch from one state to another. This lets you control your code based on the current state of the game.

- **Spawn Point**: When the player taps the screen, the game adds an AR anchor in the camera's view. A tiny box that acts as the spawning point for the emojis also appears.

- **Error Handling**: Your game is robust enough to handle whatever the real world can throw at it. It informs the player of any tracking issues and, most importantly, it can recover from an interruption.

What's next?

- **Spawning Emojis**: With the spawn point in place, you'll spawn multiple emojis at this location.

- **Running Actions**: To add some polish, you'll run some custom actions on the emojis to play sound effects, scale and run additional code.

- **Enabling Physics**: You'll enable physics so the emojis participate in the physics simulation. This gives each emoji a physical shape and applies forces like gravity to it.

- **Applying Forces**: You'll use physically-based animation to apply forces to the emojis, shooting them out from the spawning point into the world, then letting gravity pull them back to earth.

- **2D Raycasting**: You'll use 2D raycasting to check if the player touches any of the spawned emojis to save them from certain death.

Now that you know what's next, it's time to get cracking!

> **Note**: There's a copy of the final project from the previous chapter available in **starter/EmojiPop**.

Spawning emojis

Your first step is to get the emojis to spawn. You'll use the spawn point as the parent node to spawn the new emojis. This ensures the emojis spawn in the player's view.

Start by creating a helper function that spawns a single emoji. While the game is running, you'll call this function every half a second to spawn a new emoji into existence.

Open **Scene.swift**, then add the following function to `Scene`:

```
func spawnEmoji() {
  // 1
  let emojiNode = SKLabelNode(
    text:String(emojis.randomElement()!))
  emojiNode.name = "Emoji"
  emojiNode.horizontalAlignmentMode = .center
  emojiNode.verticalAlignmentMode = .center
  // 2
```

```
  guard let sceneView = self.view as? ARSKView else { return }
  let spawnNode = sceneView.scene?.childNode(
    withName: "SpawnPoint")
  spawnNode?.addChild(emojiNode)
}
```

This defines a function named spawnEmoji() whose main responsibility is spawning a single emoji.

Take a closer look at what it's doing:

1. Creates a new SKLabelNode using a random emoji character from the string of emojis available in emojis. The node is named **Emoji** and it's centered vertically and horizontally.

2. Interrogates the available node in scene, looking for the node named SpawnPoint. It then adds the newly-created emoji as a child of spawnNode. This places the emoji into the scene.

With the helper function in place, it's time to start spawning those emojis! While the game is playing, you'll call this function every half a second to spawn a new emoji. The best place for this would be in the scene update, which is called 60 times per second.

Add the following to update(_:):

```
// 1
if gameState != .Playing { return }
// 2
if spawnTime == 0 { spawnTime = currentTime + 3 }
// 3
if spawnTime < currentTime {
  spawnEmoji()
  spawnTime = currentTime + 0.5;
}
//4
updateHUD("SCORE: " + String(score) +
  " | LIVES: " + String(lives))
```

Here's how this breaks down:

1. You only want to update the game while it's in the **Playing** state.

2. If `spawnTime` is `0`, the game just started so you give the player a few seconds to prepare for the onslaught of emojis that are about to spawn. This creates a slight delay of 3 seconds before the first emoji spawns.

3. Once `spawnTime` is less than `currentTime`, it's time to spawn a new emoji. Once spawned, you reset `spawnTime` to wait for another half a second before spawning the next emoji.

4. Finally, you update the HUD with the current score and available lives.

Great, you're finally spawning emojis! You're welcome to do a quick build and run to test things out, but prepare to be underwhelmed.

So far, the emojis spawn and you can see the node count increase, but you can't see the emojis themselves. That's because they're hiding behind the spawn point.

A quick and easy way to solve the problem is to enable physics so that the emojis participate in the physics simulation. Once spawned, gravity will pull the emojis toward the ground.

Enabling physics

SpriteKit comes with a very powerful 2D physics engine. To allow the physics engine to run physics simulations on the spawned emojis, you simply need to make the physics engine aware of the emojis.

To enable physics, you need to attach a **physics body** to the SpriteKit node. The physics body describes all the physical properties of the node, including their shape, mass, friction, damping and restitution.

The physics engine will take all this information into account when it simulates 2D physics interactions on the nodes. Those interactions include things like gravity, friction and collisions with other nodes in the physical world.

Physics body types

One of the key properties you must specify when creating a physics body is its **type**. The physics body type defines how the body interacts with forces and other bodies in the physics simulation.

SpriteKit uses three types of physics bodies:

- **Dynamic**: The physics engine automatically moves this type of body in response to forces and collisions.

- **Static**: This type of body is similar to a dynamic body, except that the physics engine ignores its velocity and forces and collisions don't affect it. You can still move and rotate these types of bodies, and other dynamic bodies will interact with it.

- **Edge**: This type of body is very similar to a static body, but it has no volume. Use edges to represent negative space within a scene, such as an invisible boundary.

Physics shapes

In addition to the type, **shape** is another important property you must specify when creating a physics body. This defines the 2D shape the physics engine uses to detect collisions.

When choosing a shape to use, there's usually a tradeoff between performance and the accuracy of the collisions.

Take careful note of the following spaceship, with various examples of physics body shapes indicated in gray.

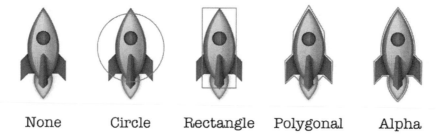

None   Circle   Rectangle   Polygonal   Alpha

When creating a physics body, SpriteKit allows you to use the following shapes:

- **None**: This allows you to demonstrate a node with no physics body attached.

- **Circular**: This is the most performant physics shape to use. It defines a circular volume around the spaceship, which the physics engine uses for collisions. Although you'll get the best possible performance, the collisions won't be very accurate.

- **Rectangular**: This is the second most performant physics shape to use. It defines a rectangular volume around the spaceship. Although this shape produces better results during collisions, it's still not very accurate when considering the shape of the spaceship.

- **Polygonal**: There's a significant performance hit when using this type of physics shape. It does, however, allow you to define a polygonal volume around the spaceship that matches the shape more accurately. You'll get more accurate collisions, but at a cost.

- **Alpha Channel**: This is the most expensive shape type to use. It uses the image alpha channel to calculate a volume around the spaceship. You'll get pixel-perfect collisions, producing highly accurate results, but at a very high performance cost.

Now that you've covered the basics, it's time to enable physics on the spawned emojis.

Enabling physics

In SpriteKit, all physics bodies are SKPhysicsBody objects. Once you create a physics body, you assign it to the physicsBody property of the SKNode.

Add the following to the bottom of spawnEmoji():

```
// Enable Physics
emojiNode.physicsBody = SKPhysicsBody(circleOfRadius: 15)
emojiNode.physicsBody?.mass = 0.01
```

This creates a new, circular-shaped physics body that you'll attach to the emoji node's physicsBody. The physical mass of the body is set to 10 grams.

Build and run. Now, you'll notice something different from before.

When the emojis spawn, they start to fall towards the ground. You've applied a gravitational force to them by having them participate in the physics simulation.

This is a good step forward, but you still want to make the game more exciting.

Force

In real life, when you want to make a ball move, you have to apply a force to it — by kicking it, for example. Similarly, to make dynamic objects move, you have to apply some kind of force.

A force has both a magnitude and direction. You define these as a 2D vector containing an X- and Y-axis:

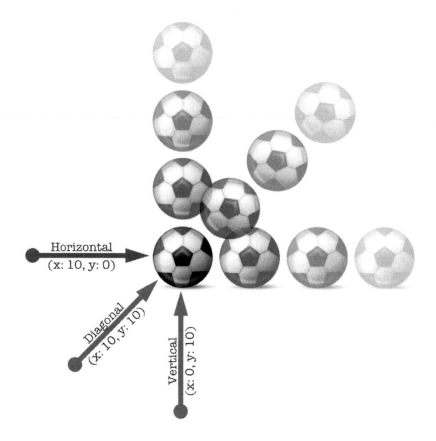

These examples show various forces applied to the ball and the resulting reaction:

- **Horizontal**: Applying a 2D force vector of (x: 10, y: 0) will push the ball to the right horizontally.

- **Vertical**: Applying a 2D force vector of (x: 0, y: 10) will push the ball upwards vertically.

- **Diagonal**: Applying a 2D force vector of (x: 10, y: 10) will push the ball diagonally, moving upwards and right at the same time.

Adding some randomness

Adding some randomness to the gameplay will make the game more challenging and increase the replay value. Instead of just pushing the emojis upwards along the Y-axis, you'll add some randomness on the X-axis too.

Add the following helper function to Scene:

```
func randomCGFloat() -> CGFloat {
  return CGFloat(Float(arc4random()) / Float(UINT32_MAX))
}
```

This function will generate a random value between `0.0` and `1.0`. Now, you can easily bring in some randomness when applying force to the emojis.

Applying an impulse

Instead of applying a constant force, you'll apply the force as an impulse. Gravity, for example, is a constant force, whereas a kick is an impulse.

To apply an impulse, use `applyImpulse()`, which is available on the `physicsBody` of the `SKNode`.

Add the following to the bottom of `spawnEmoji()`:

```
// Add Impulse
emojiNode.physicsBody?.applyImpulse(CGVector(
  dx: -5 + 10 * randomCGFloat(), dy: 10))
```

This applies an impulse on the emoji's physics body, kicking it upwards with a random sideways direction.

Torque

Torque is another type of force that you can apply to physics bodies — a rotational force. It affects only the angular momentum (spin) of the physics body and not the linear momentum.

Applying torque will make the node spin around its center of mass.

No Torque   +Torque   -Torque

To make the node spin to the right, apply a positive torque to the physics body. When you apply a negative torque, the node will spin to the left.

Applying torque

You can use `applyTorque()`, which is available on the `physicsBody`, to apply torque to a `SKNode`.

Add the following to the bottom of `spawnEmoji()`:

```
// Add Torque
emojiNode.physicsBody?.applyTorque(-0.2 + 0.4 * randomCGFloat())
```

This applies a torque to the emoji's physics body, making it in a random direction.

Another build and run will show you the current state of affairs.

The emojis no longer just fall. They're shot up into the air at random trajectories, then they fall to their doom. Awesome! But hang on, there's more you can do to spice up the game, but you need to know a little bit about actions and how to run them first.

Actions

Actions allow you to perform basic animations to manipulate a node's position, scale, rotation and opacity within a scene. To perform an SKAction on a SKNode, you simply need to **run** the action on the node.

Here are a few transformative SKActions available:

- **Scale**: If you want to grow tiny Coolio into big Coolio when he collects a power-up, use the scale action.

- **Move**: If you want to jump over an enemy when the player performs a certain action, there's a move action to do it.

- **Fade**: You just drank a magic potion that turns you into a translucent ghost, thanks to the fade action.

- **Rotate**: If you want to roll forward and squish a bug when the player performs an action, use the rotate action.

> **Note**: Be aware that if the node has a dynamic physics body attached, you should not run transformative actions on it. If the node is declared as a static physics body, then you're good to go. Fading a node in and out should be fine, too.

Here are a few special `SKActions`:

- **Wait**: If you want to pause for a moment before performing another action, use the wait action.
- **Remove from Parent**: If you want to destroy a squished bug and make it disappear from the scene, there's a handy remove from parent action you can use.
- **Play Sound**: If you want the squished bug to scream while it's being crushed, use play sound to give it its last words.
- **Run Code Block**: If you want to execute custom code after running some actions, there's a run code block action you can use. This is super useful for injecting conditional code into action sequences.

Sequence & group actions

You can run only run a single `SKAction` on a `SKNode` at a time, but there are two special types of actions you can use to run multiple actions in a **sequence** or in a **group**.

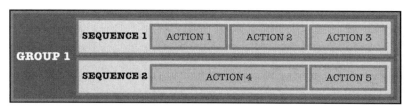

In the illustration above, consider the following:

- **Actions 1 - 5**: There are five basic actions. For demonstration purposes, say each action will take one second to complete, except action 4, which will take two seconds.

- **Sequences 1 - 2**: A **sequence action** contains multiple actions that run one by one in sequence. Sequence 1 contains actions 1 to 3, which will take three seconds to complete. Sequence 2 contains actions 4 and 5, which will also take three seconds to complete.

- **Group 1**: A **group action** allows you to group actions together so they can run in parallel. Because group 1 consists of two sequence actions, the resulting group action will run as follows: Sequences 1 and 2 trigger at the same time. Actions 1 and 2 run in sequence, and action 4 runs at the same time. Finally, after actions 1, 2 and 4 complete, actions 3 and 5 run at the same time.

Adding sound files

In the next section, you're going to use a play sound action to add some fun noises to your game. To do this, you'll need to add a few sound files to your project.

Drag and drop the entire **SoundEffects** folder, located under **starter/resources**, into your project.

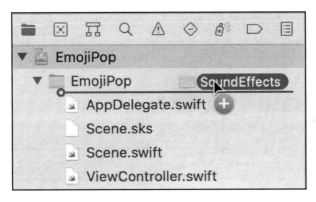

Be sure to enable **Copy Items If Needed** with the target set to **EmojiPop**, then select **Finish** to complete the process.

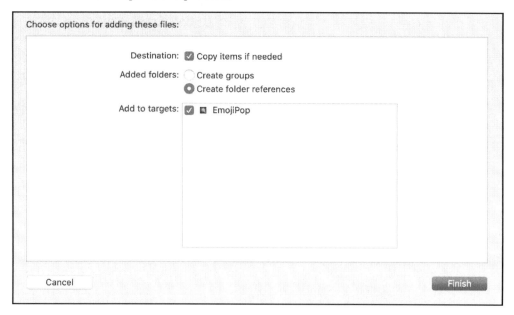

This adds the audio resources to your project. You'll reference them when you play sound effects.

Running actions

Now that you know all about actions, you'll bring the game to life by adding some actions to it.

Add the following to the bottom of `spawnEmoji()`:

```
// 1
let spawnSoundAction = SKAction.playSoundFileNamed(
    "SoundEffects/Spawn.wav", waitForCompletion: false)
let dieSoundAction = SKAction.playSoundFileNamed(
    "SoundEffects/Die.wav", waitForCompletion: false)
let waitAction = SKAction.wait(forDuration: 3)
let removeAction = SKAction.removeFromParent()
// 2
let runAction = SKAction.run({
  self.lives -= 1
  if self.lives <= 0 {
    self.stopGame()
  }
})
```

```
// 3
let sequenceAction = SKAction.sequence(
  [spawnSoundAction, waitAction, dieSoundAction, runAction,
    removeAction])
emojiNode.run(sequenceAction)
```

Here's how this breaks down:

1. Creates a few basic actions that you'll use in just a moment. They're fairly self-explanatory based on their names and action types.

2. Creates a custom code block action that decreases the lives by one. When all the lives are depleted, the game stops.

3. Creates a single action sequence that consists of all the previously-created actions. You then run the sequence action against the freshly-spawned emojis. The resulting action sequence will play out as follows, as soon as an emoji is spawned: **Play spawn sound ▸ Wait for three seconds ▸ Play die sound ▸ Decrease lives / stop game ▸ Remove emojis from scene**.

This will automatically manage the spawned emojis. If the player fails to save them in time, the game automatically removes them and considers them dead. So sad. :[

Build and run to see how things look now.

The emojis spawn with a nice squeaky sound, then fall to their deaths. You can even hear them hit the ground with a thud, causing you to lose a life and, eventually, lose the game.

Understanding 2D raycasting

The poor emojis, there's no way to save them right now. That's just so sadistically… satisfying! :]

Bring out the hero in yourself and let **2D raycasting** come to the rescue, saving the day and, of course, millions of emojis.

So how does 2D raycasting work?

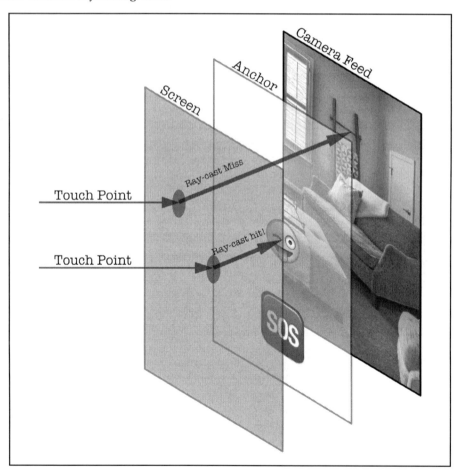

When the player touches the screen, which is a two-dimensional surface, the game has to convert that touch point into three-dimensional space to determine if the player touched a node.

To do that, a **ray** is **cast** from the phone's physical position into augmented space to that touched location on the screen. When the ray hits a node, that node is reported as a touched node. If the ray doesn't hit anything, the player missed.

Handling touches

Next, you'll add touch functionality to the game so the player can save those poor emojis.

Add the following helper function to Scene:

```swift
func checkTouches(_ touches: Set<UITouch>) {
  // 1
  guard let touch = touches.first else { return }
  let touchLocation = touch.location(in: self)
  let touchedNode = self.atPoint(touchLocation)
  // 2
  if touchedNode.name != "Emoji" { return }
  score += 1
  // 3
  let collectSoundAction = SKAction.playSoundFileNamed(
      "SoundEffects/Collect.wav", waitForCompletion: false)
  let removeAction = SKAction.removeFromParent()
  let sequenceAction = SKAction.sequence(
    [collectSoundAction, removeAction])
  touchedNode.run(sequenceAction)
}
```

This defines a function called checkTouches(_:) that checks if the player touched an emoji.

Take a look at what's happening here:

1. This takes the first available touch from a provided list of touches. It then uses the touched screen location to do a quick raycast into the scene, determining whether the player hit any of the available SKNodes.

2. If the player touched a node, and it's indeed an emoji node, the score increases by 1.

3. Finally, you create and run an action sequence consisting of a sound effect and an action that will remove the emoji node from its parent node — ultimately destroying the touched emoji by removing it from the scene.

With this function in place, find and uncomment the call to it in `touchesBegan_:with:)`:

```
checkTouches(touches)
```

While the game is running, you'll check if the player touched any emojis, then remove them from the scene.

Fantastic, you can now save those emojis! You're almost done, there's just one tiny thing left to do.

Adding finishing touches

When the game starts, the spawn point just pops into view. This feels a bit abrupt and unpolished. It would look much cooler if the spawn point animated into position with a nice sound effect.

Open **ViewController.swift**, then find `view(_:nodeFor:)` and change the initial 'boxNode' scale from `1.5` to `0`, as follows:

```
boxNode.setScale(0)
```

Now, when the game creates the box, it's so small that it's invisible.

Add the following to the bottom of `view(_:nodeFor:)`, right before `return`:

```
let startSoundAction = SKAction.playSoundFileNamed(
  "SoundEffects/GameStart.wav", waitForCompletion: false)
let scaleInAction = SKAction.scale(to: 1.5, duration: 0.8)
boxNode.run(SKAction.sequence(
  [startSoundAction, scaleInAction]))
```

This creates and runs an action sequence consisting of a sound effect and a scale effect on the created box node. It slowly scales the box to `1.5` while playing a nice sound effect.

Great! See how easy it is to add polish using just basic actions?

You're all done! Build and run your game and reap the rewards of all your effort.

You've just finished your awesome SpriteKit-based ARKit game!

Key points

Congratulations, you've reached the end of the chapter and section.

While you soak in this proud moment, here's a quick recap of all the things you learned in this chapter:

- **Physics**: You now know how to enable physics on nodes. This is an easy way to breathe life into your AR content. You can make objects interact with one another using collisions, manipulate them with linear-based forces and even make them spin by applying torque.
- **Actions**: Actions are incredibly powerful, enabling you to do all sorts of things like move, scale and rotate nodes. You can play sounds, remove nodes from scenes and run custom code blocks. You can run them in a sequence or in a group.
- **2D Raycasting**: Finding touched nodes is as easy as taking the screen touch point and doing a raycast into the scene to see if it hits any nodes.

In the next chapter, you'll learn about using SceneKit with ARKit. Now, go challenge your friends and family to see who can save the most emojis. See you soon!

Section VI: ARKit & SceneKit

In this section, you'll continue learning about ARKit. You'll also learn about SceneKit, Apple's framework for creating 3D content, as you build a miniature interactive virtual airport that allows customers to access basic departure and arrivals information.

Chapter 15: ARKit & SceneKit

Now that you've seen ARKit in action alongside Apple's general-purpose 2D graphics framework, SpriteKit, it's time to unlock the third dimension with SceneKit. In this chapter, you'll continue to learn more about ARKit, but with the focus of using it with SceneKit as its rendering technology.

You'll start by creating a new SceneKit-based AR project with Xcode. The project will grow into an interactive 3D augmented reality experience: a small AR Airport with basic animations.

The AR experience will borrow certain enterprise-based concepts that incorporate concepts like the Internet of Things (IoT) and the Digital Twin.

Don't worry, the data component for this project is non-existent. Your main focus is to create an awesome AR experience that will serve as a fun little frontend.

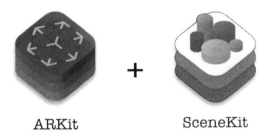

ARKit + SceneKit

What is SceneKit?

SceneKit is a high-performance rendering engine and 3D graphics framework. It's built on top of Metal, which delivers the highest performance possible. It leverages the power of Swift to deliver a simple, yet extremely powerful and descriptive, 3D graphics framework. With it, you can easily import, manipulate and render 3D content. With its built-in physics simulation and animation capabilities, creating rich 3D experiences has never been easier.

Best of all, Apple's platforms all support SceneKit and it integrates extremely well with other frameworks, like GameplayKit and SpriteKit.

Creating a SceneKit AR project

Start Xcode — it's time to create a SceneKit-based AR project.

Create a new project in **Xcode** and, when asked to select your template, choose **iOS ▸ Application ▸ Augmented Reality App**, then click **Next** to continue.

Change the **Product Name** to **ARPort** and choose **SceneKit** for the **Content Technology**. You'll use a **Storyboard** UI, so leave the **Interface** as-is and leave the **Language** as **Swift**.

Finally, turn off **Include Tests** and click **Next** to continue.

Xcode now generates a bare-bones SceneKit-based Augmented Reality project for you.

Let it finish and, before doing anything else, take the app for a quick spin. Build and run the project to see what the bare-bones app does out of the box.

When the app starts, it uses the phone's current position in real-world space as the world origin point. It then spawns a big spaceship at that exact position. You'll need to take a step back to see it fully. My oh my, so shiny! :]

Now, take a moment to explore the contents of the project.

Exploring the project

In Xcode, with the project open, explore the important components that Xcode generated for you based on the **SceneKit Augmented Reality Template** project. Although the generated project is similar to a SpriteKit project, there are a few small differences:

AppDelegate.swift

This is the standard starting point of your app.

LaunchScreen.storyboard

The launch screen is a standard part of every app. It's the first thing the user sees when the app launches. Here, you'll represent your app with a beautiful splash image.

Main.storyboard

The main storyboard is the view component of your AR app, containing the app's UI. This is a good place to put buttons and heads-up displays, for example.

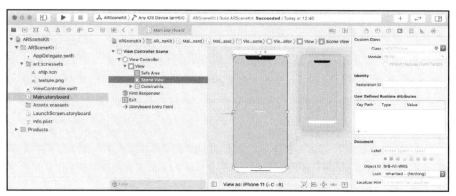

Take particular note of the `ARSCNView` scene view class, which lets you overlay an AR scene over a live background image feed from the camera. It provides seamless integration between ARKit and SceneKit. Also, note that the view is connected to an `@IBOutlet` defined in **ViewController.swift**.

ViewController.swift

The view controller contains the code behind the entire AR experience, specifically the main storyboard.

Take note of the frameworks at play:

- **UIKit**: Contains the required infrastructure for iOS and tvOS apps, including the window and view architecture to implement the UI, event handling and input. It also provides support for animation, document, drawing, printing, device information, text and display, search, accessibility, app extension and resource management.

- **SceneKit**: Supports 3D graphics.

- **ARKit**: Provides ARKit support.

The `ViewController` inherits directly from the standard `UIViewController`, which provides the infrastructure for managing the views of a basic UIKit-based app.

It also adopts the `ARSCNViewDelegate` protocol from ARKit, which contains methods you can implement to synchronize your SceneKit content with your AR session.

Take special note of `@IBOutlet`. It connects to `ARSCNView`, which is defined in the **Main.storyboard**.

Look at `viewDidLoad()`, where the app loads and presents the default `SCNScene` scene named **scene**.

`viewWillAppear(_:)` is where you create an `ARWorldTrackingConfiguration` instance. This configuration is provided to the view's `ARSession` when the user starts the app.

art.scnassets

art.scnassets is a standard folder that was simply renamed by adding the **.scnassets** extension to it. This type of folder is known as a **SceneKit Asset Catalog**. Its purpose is to help you manage your game assets separately from the code.

Xcode will copy the contents of this folder to your app bundle at build time. Xcode will also preserve the folder hierarchy, giving you full control over the folder structure.

ship.scn

Within the SceneKit Asset Catalog, you'll find a **b** file. This defines the **SceneKit Scene** containing a model of the ship that you see when the AR experience starts.

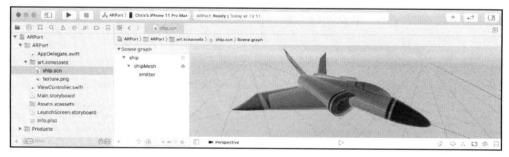

The view controller loads and presents this scene.

Assets.xcassets

Here, you find your standard app assets like your app icon, for example.

Info.plist

When your app runs for the first time, it needs to ask for permission to access the camera. ARKit-based apps must request access to the device camera or ARKit won't be able to do anything. It does this by setting the value of **Privacy — Camera Usage Description**.

Loading & exploring the Starter project

Now that you know how to create a standard SceneKit-based AR project with Xcode… you won't use the project you just created.

To speed things up a bit, you'll use a specially prepared project instead, which already has a few basic housekeeping things done for you. This way, you can focus on the important ARKit- and SceneKit-related tasks.

Get started by opening **ARPort.xcodeproj** in the **Starter** folder and checking out a few important components you need to know.

ViewController.swift

You'll find that the view controller has been reduced to its bare bones. Don't worry, you'll fill in all the missing code later.

You'll also find a few important stubs within the code. These act as sections, separating the code into clear, manageable blocks that deal with specific parts of your app. They'll also make it easier to locate the correct places to enter code as you work through the tutorial.

Here's a quick breakdown of some of the important sections you'll find:

- **App State Management**: Plays a key part in managing your app through various states.
- **Properties**: You define all class variable members here.
- **IB Outlets**: Gives you quick access to some key UI elements because they're already connected to **Main.storyboard**.
- **IB Actions**: These actions have also been connected to **Main.storyboard**. You'll call these methods when the user interacts with button elements or makes a gesture.

- **App Management**: Dedicated to methods related to managing the app through its entire lifecycle.

- **AR Coaching Overlay**: Used to create and manage an AR Coaching Overlay. More on this in just a minute.

- **AR Session Management**: Focuses on managing the AR session, along with handling possible issues and errors.

- **Scene Management**: Focuses on SceneKit scene management.

- **Focus Node Management**: Manages the Focus Node. More on what that is in the next chapter.

Main.storyboard

Next, you'll look at **Main.storyboard**.

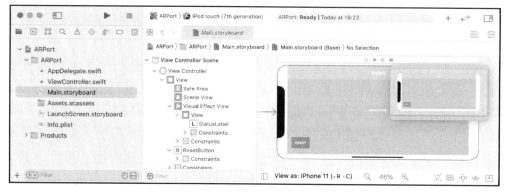

Of particular interest are these three elements of the storyboard:

- **StatusLabel**: At the top of the screen, located within a Visual Effect view that blurs the background, you'll find the status label that you'll use to keep the user informed at all times. This UI element connects to the `statusLabel` variable within the view controller.

- **ResetButton**: Located at the bottom left of the screen, this button will reset the AR experience. This UI element connects to `resetButtonPressed()` within the view controller.

- **TapGesture**: A tap gesture recognizer that triggers `tapGestureHandler()` when the user taps the screen.

App state management

With all the logistics out of the way, you'll start with some basic app management. The app requires a state machine to manage its lifecycle through various states. During each individual state, the app will focus on doing one particular thing.

Open **ViewController.swift** and add the following enum to the **App State Management** section:

```
enum AppState: Int16 {
  case DetectSurface
  case PointAtSurface
  case TapToStart
  case Started
}
```

The enum will manage the app through the following states:

- **DetectSurface**: During this state, the AR session will actively detect viable horizontal surfaces, known as **planes**.

- **PointAtSurface**: The AR session has now successfully detected viable horizontal surfaces. Now, the user has to point towards the detected surface so a focus node can appear.

- **TapToStart**: The user is pointing towards a viable surface and the focus node is visible. The focus node acts as a visual indicator, showing the user where the 3D content will appear when the AR experience starts.

- **Started**: The user placed the 3D content and the AR experience has started. The user is now interacting with the 3D content in AR.

With the enum in place, add the following variables under the **Properties** section of the view controller class:

```
var trackingStatus: String = ""
var statusMessage: String = ""
var appState: AppState = .DetectSurface
```

You'll use `appState` to keep track of the current active state. Both `trackingStatus` and `statusMessage` will help keep the user informed. You'll use them to show the current AR tracking status along with an instructional message so the user knows what to do at all times.

With the basic app state in place, it's time to add the following helper functions under the **App Management** section:

```
// 1
func startApp() {
  DispatchQueue.main.async {
    self.appState = .DetectSurface
  }
}
//2
func resetApp() {
  DispatchQueue.main.async {
    //self.resetARSession()
    self.appState = .DetectSurface
  }
}
```

Here's what these functions do:

1. Sets the `appState` to `DetectSurface`. As mentioned above, the AR session will actively detect planes in this state.

2. Resets the AR session, which is currently commented out. You'll uncomment its code after you create that function. It also sets the `appState` to `DetectSurface`.

Basic scene management

Now, move on to the SceneKit component of your app. The first thing you need to do is to make the view controller comply with a special protocol.

Add the `ARSCNViewDelegate` protocol to `ViewController` so the class definition looks like this:

```
class ViewController: UIViewController, ARSCNViewDelegate {
```

`ARSCNViewDelegate` provides various methods to update your **SceneKit** content. These methods correspond to `ARAnchor` objects, which the AR session is tracking. This comes in handy when you want to manage detected surfaces that are represented as planes, for example.

Initializing a new SceneKit scene

Now, to create the new SceneKit scene.

Add the following function to the **Scene Management** section:

```
func initScene() {
  // 1
  let scene = SCNScene()
  sceneView.scene = scene
  // 2
  sceneView.delegate = self
}
```

Creating a new scene is really easy:

1. You create a new `SCNScene` instance, which you then set to the scene view's scene.

2. You then set the view controller as the scene view's delegate, which now conforms to `ARSCNViewDelegate`.

Excellent! Now that you've created the scene, you'll provide the user with some helpful information.

Providing feedback

Feedback helps the user know what the app is doing and what steps they need to take next. To start providing feedback, add the following helper function to the **Scene Management** section:

```
func updateStatus() {
  // 1
  switch appState {
  case .DetectSurface:
    statusMessage = "Scan available flat surfaces..."
  case .PointAtSurface:
    statusMessage = "Point at designated surface first!"
  case .TapToStart:
    statusMessage = "Tap to start."
  case .Started:
    statusMessage = "Tap objects for more info."
  }
  // 2
  self.statusLabel.text = trackingStatus != "" ?
      "\(trackingStatus)" : "\(statusMessage)"
}
```

This helper function keeps the user informed by:

1. Setting a `statusMessage` based on the current app state.
2. Constructing the final status label's message for the user by combining `trackingStatus` and `statusMessage`.

To put this helper function to good use, add the following function to the **Scene Management** section:

```
func renderer(_ renderer: SCNSceneRenderer,
  updateAtTime time: TimeInterval) {
  DispatchQueue.main.async {
    self.updateStatus()
  }
}
```

SceneKit calls `renderer(_:updateAtTime:)` once for every frame update. This ensures that `updateStatus()` is called regularly, keeping the user constantly informed.

> **Note**: By calling `updateStatus()` inside `DispatchQueue.main.async`, you ensure the call executes within the main thread. This is very important when updating any information located on the UI. If you don't, you might experience some update lag.

Now, to ensure the scene actually initializes when the app starts, add a call to it at the bottom of `viewDidLoad()`:

```
self.initView()
```

Great, now the scene will initialize when the app starts. This is a great time to test everything out. Build and run to deploy the app to your device.

Fantastic, the app started and the scene initialized… but it's totally dark! That's because you haven't started ARKit yet. You'll look at that component next.

AR session management

Now that you've created the scene and ensured that the user will be kept informed of what the app's doing, move on to the AR component.

Main.storyboard contains `ARSCNView`, which is basically a `SceneKit` view. It includes `ARSession`, which is responsible for motion tracking and image processing in ARKit. It's session-based, which means you have to create an AR session instance, then you have to run that session to start the AR tracking process.

AR configuration

Before starting an AR session, you have to create an AR session configuration. You use this configuration to establish the connection between the real world, where your device is, and the virtual 3D world, where your virtual content is.

There are six types of configurations:

- **AROrientationTrackingConfiguration**: Basic three degrees of freedom (3DOF) tracking.

- **ARWorldTrackingConfiguration**: Six degrees of freedom (6DOF) tracking. Tt also tracks people, known images and objects.

- **ARBodyTrackingConfiguration**: Tracks human bodies.

- **ARImageTrackingConfiguration**: Tracks known images.

- **ARObjectScanningConfiguration**: Tracks known 3D objects.

- **ARFaceTrackingConfiguration**: Tracks faces and facial expressions using the front-facing camera.

Starting the AR session

With **ViewController.swift** still open, add the following extension under the **AR Session Management** section:

```
func initARSession() {
  // 1
  guard ARWorldTrackingConfiguration.isSupported else {
    print("*** ARConfig: AR World Tracking Not Supported")
    return
  }
  // 2
  let config = ARWorldTrackingConfiguration()
  // 3
  config.worldAlignment = .gravity
  config.providesAudioData = false
  config.planeDetection = .horizontal
  config.isLightEstimationEnabled = true
  config.environmentTexturing = .automatic
  // 4
  sceneView.session.run(config)
}
```

Take a look at what's happening here:

1. `isSupported` checks if the device supports the required AR configuration. This is a good time to tell the user to upgrade their iPhone, if necessary! :]

2. Creates an `ARWorldTrackingConfiguration` configuration instance assigned to `config`. This gives your app six degrees of freedom (6DOF) tracking, as well as tracking people, known images and objects.

3. This sets a few configuration requirements:

   a) **worldAlignment**: Setting it to **gravity** sets the coordinate system's y-axis parallel to gravity, with the origin to the initial position of the device.

   b) **providesAudioData**: This disables capturing audio during the AR session. You don't want to sample any audio.

   c) **planeDetection**: You set it to **horizontal**, which specifies that the AR session should automatically detect horizontal flat surfaces. More on this in just a second.

d) **isLightEstimationEnabled**: By setting this to **true**, you give the running AR session responsibility for providing scene lighting information.

e) **environmentTexturing**: Setting this to **automatic** lets the AR session automatically determine when and where to generate environment textures.

4. Finally, this calls `run(_:options:)` on `ARSCNView`'s `ARSession`, passing in the freshly created `ARWorldTrackingConfiguration`. This ultimately starts the AR session.

Resetting the AR session

At times, you might want to reset the AR session. This comes in handy when you want to restart the AR experience, for example.

To do this, add the following function to the **AR Session Management** section:

```
func resetARSession() {
  // 1
  let config = sceneView.session.configuration as!
    ARWorldTrackingConfiguration
  // 2
  config.planeDetection = .horizontal
  // 3
  sceneView.session.run(config,
    options: [.resetTracking, .removeExistingAnchors])
}
```

Here's how it breaks down:

1. You can gain access to the existing AR configuration through the AR session configuration. This casts the existing AR configuration back into an `ARWordTrackingConfiguration`.

2. This ensures that **planeDection** is still set to **horizontal** so the AR session will continue to automatically detect horizontal flat surfaces once it resets.

3. Finally, this resets the AR session with the following options:

   a) **resetTracking**: Simply resets the device's position from the previous session run.

   b) **removeExistingAnchors**: Removes all the anchor objects associated with the previous session run.

Handling AR session state changes

Now that you can start and reset the AR session, you need to keep the user informed any time the AR session state changes. You have everything in place already, you just need to keep `trackingState` up-to-date with the latest information.

Add the following function override to the **AR Session Management** section:

```
func session(_ session: ARSession,
  cameraDidChangeTrackingState camera: ARCamera) {
  switch camera.trackingState {
  case .notAvailable: self.trackingStatus =
    "Tracking: Not available!"
  case .normal: self.trackingStatus = ""
  case .limited(let reason):
    switch reason {
    case .excessiveMotion: self.trackingStatus =
      "Tracking: Limited due to excessive motion!"
    case .insufficientFeatures: self.trackingStatus =
      "Tracking: Limited due to insufficient features!"
    case .relocalizing: self.trackingStatus =
      "Tracking: Relocalizing..."
    case .initializing: self.trackingStatus =
      "Tracking: Initializing..."
    @unknown default: self.trackingStatus =
      "Tracking: Unknown..."
    }
  }
}
```

This interrogates the camera's current tracking state and populates `trackingState` with an appropriate message to show the user.

Handling AR session issues

Finally, you need to keep the user informed when any issues occur. Again, you'll use `trackingState` for this purpose.

Add the following function overrides to the **AR Session Management** section:

```
func session(_ session: ARSession,
  didFailWithError error: Error) {
  self.trackingStatus = "AR Session Failure: \(error)"
}

func sessionWasInterrupted(_ session: ARSession) {
  self.trackingStatus = "AR Session Was Interrupted!"
}
```

```
func sessionInterruptionEnded(_ session: ARSession) {
  self.trackingStatus = "AR Session Interruption Ended"
}
```

Once any of these session issues occur, `trackingState` is populated with an appropriate message that will be displayed to the user.

Now, to make sure the AR session actually initializes when the app starts, add a call to it at the bottom of `viewDidLoad()`:

```
self.initARSession()
```

Also, connect the **Reset** button by adding the following line of code to `resetButtonPressed(_:)`:

```
self.resetARSession()
```

Finally, uncomment the call to `resetARSession(_:)` inside `resetApp()`.

Now, do another quick test. Build and run to see what the app looks like this time around.

The black screen has been replaced by the camera feed. That's because the AR session has been initialized and is now actively scanning for horizontal surfaces. Pressing the **Reset** button will also work, restarting the tracking when you press it.

Excellent, you're making great progress!

AR Coaching Overlay

Currently, the app uses the status bar at the top to provide step-by-step instructions to help onboard the user into the AR experience. However, your approach to this onboarding process might differ entirely from another developer's. This causes massive fragmentation in AR experiences as the user switches from one experience to another.

Apple is curbing this fragmentation with the **AR Coaching Overlay View**.

What is an AR Coaching Overlay view?

Apple now provides a special overlay view known as the `ARCoachingOverlayView`. You can easily integrate it into your existing AR experiences to provide the user with a standardized AR onboarding process.

The overlay operates in a few basic states:

- **Starting State**: When the app starts, the Coaching Overlay facilitates ARKit by taking the user through a standardized onboarding process.

- **Goal-based State**: Use this to provide the overlay with a specific goal. For example, you can instruct the user to find horizontal or vertical surfaces.

- **Relocating State**: When the app loses tracking, the overlay takes over again, guiding the user back into a stable tracking state.

Pretty cool stuff! Next, you'll add it to your app.

Adding AR Coaching Overlay

The first thing to do is to ensure your view controller conforms to the new protocol.

Add the following `ARCoachingOverlayViewDelegate` protocol to the view controller under the **AR Coaching Overlay** section:

```
extension ViewController : ARCoachingOverlayViewDelegate {
}
```

And that's all it took to make the view controller conform to the new protocol.

Handling AR Coaching Overlay events

Next, you need to provide some functions to handle the overlay events.

Add the following functions to the **AR Overlay Management** section:

```
// 1
func coachingOverlayViewWillActivate(_
   coachingOverlayView: ARCoachingOverlayView) {
}
// 2
func coachingOverlayViewDidDeactivate(_
   coachingOverlayView: ARCoachingOverlayView) {
   self.startApp()
}
// 3
func coachingOverlayViewDidRequestSessionReset(_
   coachingOverlayView: ARCoachingOverlayView) {
   self.resetApp()
}
```

Here's what these functions do:

1. **coachingOverlayViewWillActivate(_:)**: This event triggers right before the overlay is activated.

2. **coachingOverlayViewDidDeactivate(_:)**: This event triggers just after the overlay is deactivated, indicating the overlay has found sufficient horizontal surfaces for the app to function. This is a great place to start the app.

3. **coachingOverlayViewDidRequestSessionReset(_:)**: This event triggers when the AR session has lost tracking for some unknown reason. The overlay will kick in again and ensure that there's sufficient horizontal surface information for the app to function. This is a great spot to reset the app so that the user can place the AR content again.

Initializing the AR Coaching Overlay

Now that you're handling everything the AR Coaching Overlay will throw at your app, you need to initialize it.

You'll do this with the following handy helper function. Add it to the **AR Coaching Overlay Management** section:

```
func initCoachingOverlayView() {
   // 1
```

```
    let coachingOverlay = ARCoachingOverlayView()
    // 2
    coachingOverlay.session = self.sceneView.session
    // 3
    coachingOverlay.delegate = self
    // 4
    coachingOverlay.activatesAutomatically = true
    // 5
    coachingOverlay.goal = .horizontalPlane
    // 6
    self.sceneView.addSubview(coachingOverlay)
}
```

Here's what it does:

1. Creates an instance of `ARCoachingOverlayView`, then stores it in `coachingOverlay`.

2. Sets the overlay's session to the same session as the scene view.

3. Sets the view controller as the overlay's delegate.

4. Configures the overlay to activate automatically. While ARKit is initializing or dealing with tracking issues, the overlay will take over and guide the user automatically. You don't have to worry about a thing.

5. Tells the overlay that you're only interested in horizontal surfaces. So the overlay will help guide the user to find horizontal surfaces during the onboarding process.

6. Finally, adds the overlay as a subview of the `sceneView` so it knows which view it needs to overlay its content.

Adding constraints to the AR Coaching Overlay

With the overlay initialized, your next step is to provide it with proper constraints.

Do this by adding the following to the bottom of `initCoachingOverlayView()`:

```
// 1
coachingOverlay.translatesAutoresizingMaskIntoConstraints =
  false
// 3
NSLayoutConstraint.activate([
  NSLayoutConstraint(item: coachingOverlay,
    attribute: .top, relatedBy: .equal,
    toItem: self.view, attribute: .top,
    multiplier: 1, constant: 0),
```

```
    NSLayoutConstraint(item: coachingOverlay,
       attribute: .bottom, relatedBy: .equal,
       toItem: self.view, attribute: .bottom,
       multiplier: 1, constant: 0),
    NSLayoutConstraint(item: coachingOverlay,
       attribute: .leading, relatedBy: .equal,
       toItem: self.view, attribute: .leading,
       multiplier: 1, constant: 0),
    NSLayoutConstraint(item: coachingOverlay,
       attribute: .trailing, relatedBy: .equal,
       toItem: self.view, attribute: .trailing,
       multiplier: 1, constant: 0)])
```

Taking a closer look, you can see it:

1. Disables the view's auto-resizing mask so it's not translated into auto layout constraints.

2. Provides the overlay with manual constraints that conform to the current view's constraints.

Great, you've now added the overlay. It will be visible when the app starts, to help guide the user through the AR onboarding process.

Finally, to ensure the AR Coaching Overlay initializes when the app starts, add a call to it at the bottom of `viewDidLoad()`:

```
self.initCoachingOverlayView()
```

Time for a final build and run. Take a look at the new AR Coaching Overlay View:

If you blink, you might have missed the AR Coaching Overlay View. Don't worry, you can make it come back. Just block the camera with your finger and the AR Coaching Overlay View should kick back into place. How cool is that? :]

> **Note**: You can find the final version of the project in **final/ARPort**.

Key points

Congratulations, you've reached the end of this chapter — and your app is shaping up nicely.

Take a look at some key points you've picked up so far:

- **SceneKit**: It's easy to create a new SceneKit-based AR experience by using Xcode's available AR app templates.
- **Key App Components**: You peeked under the hood and learned how key components play their parts in the Xcode project.
- **App State Management**: You learned how to implement basic app state management for a typical AR experience.
- **Scene Creation**: You created a blank SceneKit scene.
- **AR Session Management**: Creating, running and resetting an AR session is really simple.
- **AR Coaching Overlay View**: Making your AR experience conform to Apple's standard onboarding process is as simple as implementing an AR Coaching Overlay View into your apps.

Now, you've gotten all the groundwork out of the way. In the next chapter, you'll focus on creating the actual AR experience. See you there!

Chapter 16: Focus Nodes & Billboards

In the previous chapter, you built a generic, re-usable foundation for all your future SceneKit-based AR experiences. The app operates in a few basic states and, as an added bonus, it also conforms to a standard onboarding process thanks to Apple's AR Coaching Overlay view. This will make your users feel right at home when they pick up your app and play with the AR experiences you create.

In this chapter, you'll continue to add more components to the reusable foundation. You'll learn how to create and manage a focus node that helps the user know where content will be placed. You'll also get to build the entire AR experience with some basic interaction.

Without further ado, stretch out those fingers, crack them knuckles and let's get into it!

> **Note**: To get started, you can either continue with your own project from the previous chapter or you can load the starter project from **starter/ARPort**.

Importing 3D assets

In the previous chapter, you learned about the **SceneKit Asset Catalog**, which is a folder that your entire team of artists and developers can share. It keeps the graphics component of your app completely separate from the code. This allows you and your team to merge any graphical changes and additions into the app with minimal disruption.

Your first step to get started is to add the ready-made asset catalog to the project.

With your project open in Xcode on one side and **Finder** open on the other side, find **art.scnassets** inside **starter/resources**.

Drag and drop the **art.scnassets** folder into Xcode, placing it just above **Assets.xcassets**.

Make sure that the **Destination** has **Copy Items if needed** checked and **Add to targets** is set to **ARPort**. Select **Finish** to complete the process.

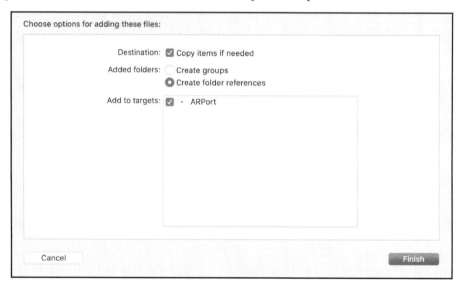

Excellent, you've successfully imported all of the 3D assets you'll need to complete the AR experience.

Focus nodes

The app already detects horizontal surfaces, so your goal now is to show the user exactly where on that surface they're pointing. This is where a focus node comes in handy.

What is a focus node?

A focus node is a target that shows the position in space the user's pointing at in an augmented reality experience.

To determine where to place the focus node, you use ray casting. A ray shoots from a focus point at the center position of the screen into augmented space. The app will place the focus node wherever the ray intersects with a previously detected surface.

Creating a focus point

Before you can create a focus point, you need to define the onscreen position to use for the ray cast. For this particular app, you'll use the center point of the screen.

You'll need to create a property to hold this center position so start by adding the following to the **Properties** section:

```
var focusPoint:CGPoint!
```

Then add the following function to the **Focus Node Management** section:

```
func initFocusNode() {
  focusPoint = CGPoint(x: view.center.x,
    y: view.center.y + view.center.y * 0.1)
}
```

This is where you'll initialize the focus node along with everything required to help manage it. You initialize the focus point at the center of the screen, with a slight 10% offset on the y-axis for a more natural feel. The ray will shoot from this screen position.

That's simple enough, but what if the user changes the screen orientation? You'll handle that issue next.

Handling orientation changes

To solve the problem, you need to update the focus point every time the user changes screen orientation.

Add the following helper function under the **Focus Node Management** section:

```
@objc
func orientationChanged() {
  focusPoint = CGPoint(x: view.center.x,
    y: view.center.y + view.center.y * 0.1)
}
```

This essentially just readjusts the focus point. Note that the function has an `@objc` attribute. This makes the function available to the `NotificationCenter`, which is part of the Objective-C runtime.

Now, you need to call the helper function when the orientation changes.

Add the following code to the bottom of `initFocusNode()`:

```
NotificationCenter.default.addObserver(self,
  selector: #selector(ViewController.orientationChanged),
  name: UIDevice.orientationDidChangeNotification,
  object: nil)
```

This notifies the app every time the orientation changes. It also calls the helper function, which updates the focus point to the correct position on the screen.

Creating a focus node

To create a new focus node, you first need to create a new SceneKit scene.

Right-click **art.scnassets/Scenes** and select **New File**.

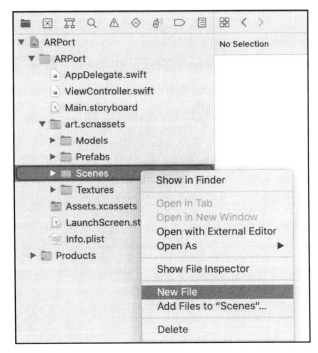

This creates a new empty scene. Rename it to **FocusScene.scn**.

With **FocusScene.scn** still open, select and delete the camera node under **Scene Graph**.

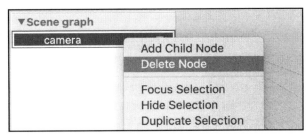

Select the + symbol at the bottom-left to add an empty node, then name it **Focus**.

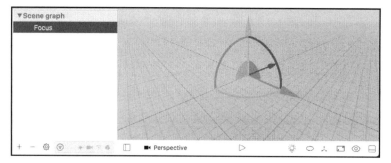

Add a new object from the **Object Library**, then search for **Plane**. Drag and drop a new **Plane** from the **Object Library** into the **Scene Graph** as a child of the **Focus** node.

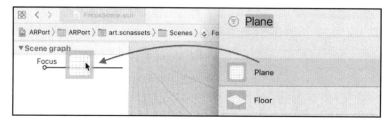

Open **art.scnassets/Textures/Focus**, then drag and drop **Footprint_DIFFUSE.png** on top of the **Footprint Plane** within the scene.

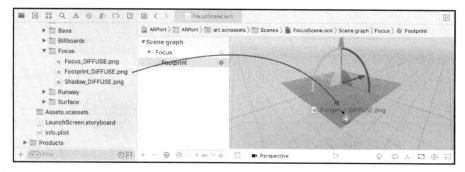

Follow the same process as before and add another **Plane** called **Shadow**, also as a child of the **Focus** node.

With the **Shadow** node selected, open the **Attributes inspector** and set the **Plane Size** to **(width: 0.15, height: 0.15)**.

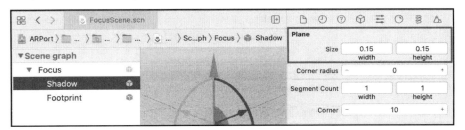

Open the **Node inspector** and set the **Transform Position** to **(x:0, y:0.001, z:0)** so the shadow is slightly above the **Footprint**, preventing z-fighting. Then drag and drop the **Shadow_DIFFUSE.png** texture onto it.

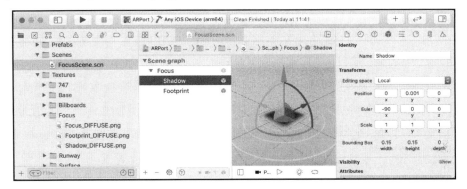

To lighten up the shadow a bit, open the **Material inspector** and set the **Settings Transparency Value** to **0.75**.

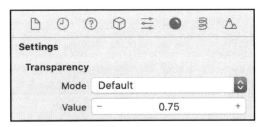

Again, follow the same process as before and drag yet another **Plane** as a child node of the **Focus** node, this time naming it **Icon**.

Set the **Plane Size** to **(width:0.1, height: 0.1)** and the **Transform Position** to **(x:0, y:0.05, z:0)**.

Finish it off by assigning the **Focus_DIFFUSE.png** texture to it. Under the Materials inspector, set its **Material Properties Shading** to **Constant**, which prevents it from reacting to light.

Here's how the result will look:

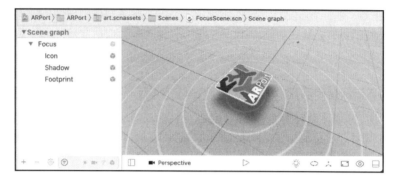

Adding billboard constraints

It would look really cool if the focus node always faced the user. To achieve that effect, you can use a **billboard constraint**. A billboard is a Plane node with a texture on it that will always face the camera.

With **FocusNode.scn** still open, select the **Focus** node, then open the **Node inspector**. Find the **Constraints** section, then select the + button to add a constraint. Select **Billboard** from the list.

Finally, you don't want the billboard constraint to affect all of the axes, only the y-axis.

Under **Constraints Settings Axes**, uncheck both the **x-axis** and the **z-axis**.

Excellent, now the focus node will always face the same direction as the user.

Loading the focus node

Now that the Focus scene is ready to go, you need to load it and add it to the main scene.

Start by creating a variable to hold the focus node. Add the following variable to the **Properties** section:

```
var focusNode: SCNNode!
```

Add the following code to the top of `initFocusNode()`:

```
// 1
let focusScene = SCNScene(
  named: "art.scnassets/Scenes/FocusScene.scn")!
// 2
focusNode = focusScene.rootNode.childNode(
  withName: "Focus", recursively: false)!
// 3
focusNode.isHidden = true
sceneView.scene.rootNode.addChildNode(focusNode)
```

Take a look at what's happening here:

1. This loads the entire **FocusScene.scn** into a local variable.

2. Now that you have a freshly loaded scene, you're only interested in the focus node. This code searches all the child nodes within the Focus scene for a node named **Focus**. Once found, it stores the node in `focusNode`.

3. Finally, you set the focus node's default state to hidden before adding it to the main scene.

With the function in place, don't forget to initialize the focus node when the app starts. To do this, add the following function call to the bottom of `viewDidLoad()`:

```
self.initFocusNode()
```

Excellent, you've now initialized the focus node.

Updating the focus node

Now that the focus node is ready to go, you need some code to manage the node's visibility.

Add the following function to the **Focus Node Management** section:

```swift
func updateFocusNode() {
  // 1
  guard appState != .Started else {
    focusNode.isHidden = true
    return
  }
  // 2
  if let query = self.sceneView.raycastQuery(
    from: self.focusPoint,
    allowing: .estimatedPlane,
    alignment: .horizontal) {
    // 3
    let results = self.sceneView.session.raycast(query)
    if results.count == 1 {
      if let match = results.first {
        // 4
        let t = match.worldTransform
        // 5
        self.focusNode.position = SCNVector3(
          x: t.columns.3.x, y: t.columns.3.y, z: t.columns.3.z)
        self.appState = .TapToStart
        focusNode.isHidden = false
      }
    } else {
      // 6
      self.appState = .PointAtSurface
      focusNode.isHidden = true
    }
  }
}
```

Quite a bit is happening in this update function:

1. For starters, the app should only update the focus node while the app's in a **Started** state. If not, the focus node state should be invisible at all times.

2. This performs a ray-cast test that shoots a virtual ray from the **focus point** outward into augmented space. It's also important to note that the ray-cast test will only consider intersections with **estimated planes** that have been identified as **horizontal** surfaces.

3. Once the test finishes, you're only interested in the first hit result.

4. You use the hit result's `worldTransform`, a transform that contains position, orientation and scale information.

5. Here, you update the focus node's position based on the hit result transform. You can find the positional information in the third column of the transform matrix. At this point, you can make the focus node visible and change the app state to **TapToStart**.

6. Ultimately, if the ray-cast test had no hit results, the app should continue to instruct the user to point at a valid surface and the focus node should be kept in a hidden state.

Now, to keep the focus node updated at all times, add the following function call in `renderer(:updateAtTime:)`:

```
self.updateFocusNode()
```

This ensures that the focus node updates once every frame.

To test the focus node, build and run.

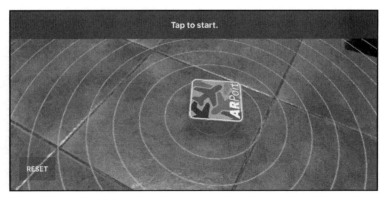

After the onboarding process, pointing toward a horizontal surface makes the focus node appear and the app switches to **TapToStart**. When you point away from the surface, the focus node will hide and the app will switch to **PointToSurface**. Excellent!

Creating the scene

Now that you know where you want to place your virtual content, it's time to create some cool content to actually place. :]

Building the scene

Create a new blank scene named **ARPortScene.scn** by right-clicking on the **art.scnassets/Scenes** folder and selecting **New File**. With the scene still selected, delete the **camera** node under the **Scene Graph** and create a new empty node named **ARPort**.

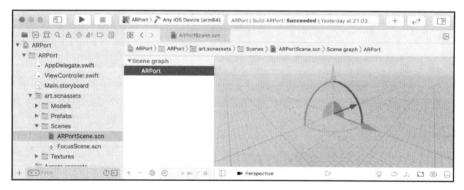

The **ARPort** node will act as the root node for the entire scene. You'll add all the elements as children of this node.

Drag and drop **art.scnassets/Models/Base.scn** into the empty space of the **Scene graph**.

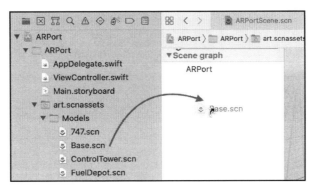

This adds the **Base.scn** scene as a reference node to the **ARPort** scene in a default position.

Finally, drag the **Base reference** node on top of the ARPort node, making it a child node.

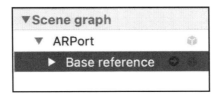

With the **Base** node selected, open the **Node inspector** and set the **Transform Position** to **(x: 0, y: 0.49, z:0)** to place the Base node on top of the ground plane.

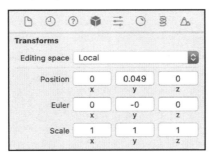

Now, follow the same process as you just did for the Base node and drag and drop the remaining nodes from **art.scnassets/Prefabs** into the **ARPortScene.scn** as children of the **ARPort** node.

Start with **Buildings.scn**, positioned at **(x: 0, y: 0.1, z:0)**.

Now, you see the main airport terminal and the control tower with its big radar.

Add **Planes.scn** next, positioned at **(x: 0, y: 0.1, z:0)**.

This adds four airplanes, one parked at each of the available terminals.

Do the same for **SolarFarm.scn**, **FuelDepots.scn** and **Trees.scn**, all positioned at **(x: 0, y: 0.1, z:0)**.

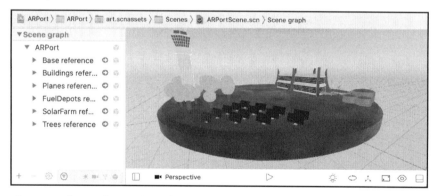

Fantastic, your airport is coming along great. But hang on, isn't something crucial still missing? Oh, of course, the runway, whoops! :]

Just like before, add **Runway.scn** and position it at **(x: 0, y: 0.1, z:0)**.

Nicely done, what a slick-looking runway; there's even a plane ready to take off.

But… you might notice the trees look a bit flat. That's because the scene still needs lighting.

Adding lights & shadows

Create a new empty node as a child of **ARPort** and name it **Lights & Shadows**. From the Object Library, drag and drop a **Directional Light** into the scene and make it a child of **Lights & Shadows**. Rename it to **DirectionalLight**, too.

Position the light at **(x: 0, y: 1, z:0)** and set the **Euler Rotation** to **(x: -75, y: 0, z:-40)**.

The trees should no longer appear flat. Instead, they're nicely lit from above, making them bright at the top and dark at the bottom. However, there's no shadow drop yet. You'll fix that next.

With **DirectionalLight** still selected, open the **Attributes inspector**. Find the **Shadow** section and check **Enable shadows** to set the directional light to cast shadows. Also, set the **Shadow Color** to a **75% Transparency** so the shadow isn't a hard black color.

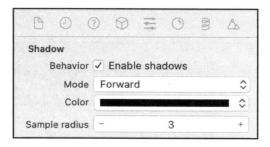

Adding a shadow catcher

To push the realism factor of your AR experience a bit, it would look amazing if the tall control tower would drop a shadow on top of the ground surface below it.

You can achieve this effect with something known as a shadow catcher. You'll add one to the scene next.

From the **Object Library**, name a Plane **ShadowCatcher** and drag and drop it into the scene as a child of **Lights & Shadows**. Under the **Attributes inspector**, set the **Plane Size** to **(width: 5, height: 5)**.

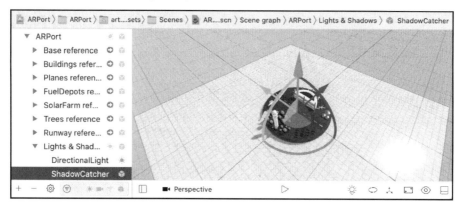

This creates a nice big, white plane that catches all of the shadows in the scene. One problem though: The plane is white, which will spoil the entire experience.

You're only interested in the shadows — the rest of the plane should be transparent. SceneKit has a special shader for just such an occasion.

With **ShadowCatcher** still selected, open the **Material inspector** and change **Properties Shading** to **Shadow Only**.

The final result will look like this:

The big white plane is now transparent, but it's catching the all-important shadows.

Loading the scene

With the scene built, you now need to do two things: First, load the scene and then, when the user taps to start the AR experience, place the ARPort at the focus node's location.

Add the following variable to the **Properties** section:

```
var arPortNode: SCNNode!
```

This creates a variable that will hold the loaded ARPort node.

Add the following block of code to the bottom of `initScene()`:

```
// 1
let arPortScene = SCNScene(
  named: "art.scnassets/Scenes/ARPortScene.scn")!
```

```
// 2
arPortNode = arPortScene.rootNode.childNode(
  withName: "ARPort", recursively: false)!
// 3
arPortNode.isHidden = true
sceneView.scene.rootNode.addChildNode(arPortNode)
```

Well, that was simple and should look familiar. It's pretty much the same process you used to load the focus node.

Nevertheless, here's a closer look:

1. Start by loading the entire **ARPortScene**.

2. Then, search for the child node named **ARPort** within the scene.

3. Set its default state to **hidden**, then add the node as a child to the main scene.

Presenting the scene

With the ARPort node ready and waiting to display, there's one thing left to do: Display the node when the user taps the screen.

Add the following code to `tapGestureHandler(_:)`:

```
// 1
guard appState == .TapToStart else { return }
// 2
self.arPortNode.isHidden = false
self.focusNode.isHidden = true
// 3
self.arPortNode.position = self.focusNode.position
// 4
appState = .Started
```

Here's what this does:

1. The app has to be in a **TapToStart** state.

2. You then set the focus node to a hidden state and the Airport node to a visible state.

3. Next, you set the Airport node's position to be the same as the focus node's.

4. Finally, progress the app state to **Started**.

What time is it? It's time to build and run that project!

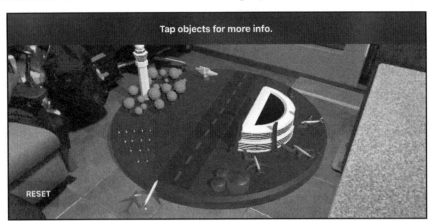

Find a space big enough, then point at the floor and let the focus node guide you. Tap to start the AR experience and stand back and be amazed. Surprise, did someone forget to mention that the scene is animated? :]

Just look at that shiny plane coming in for a landing. Don't neglect to notice its pretty shadow falling on the floor tile. Awesome!

Adding interaction

Your app is shaping up nicely, and you're almost done. But first, you'll make it a little more useful by giving the user some elements to interact with.

When the user taps on certain elements, like the runway, for example, a billboard will pop up showing the user some fake departure and arrival information.

As you learned earlier in this chapter, a billboard is a Plane node with a texture on it that will always face the camera. The effect is achieved simply by adding a **billboard** constraint to the node, similar to what you did for the focus node earlier.

Adding the billboards

To speed things up, there's a ready-made scene for you to use.

With **ARPortScene.scn** open, drag and drop **art.scnassets/Prfabs/Interaction.scn** into the **Scene graph**, then make the node a child of **ARPort**.

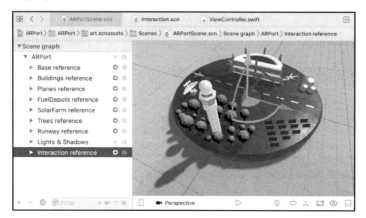

You might wonder why you're not seeing anything. That's because everything is invisible. To see what the node and its elements look like, open **art.scnassets/Prfabs/Interaction.scn**.

In the **Scene graph**, under the **Interaction** node, you'll see a whole bunch of **Touch** nodes. Select the first one and open the **Material inspector**. Then change **Properties Diffuse** to **50%** transparency.

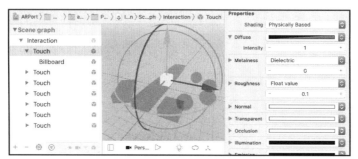

This will reveal primitive boxes and spheres that act as the interaction points. When the user touches any of these **Touch** nodes, you'll unhide the child Billboard node.

> **Note**: Don't forget to go back and set Material Properties Diffuse back to **0% transparency** when you finish testing.

Handling touch input

In **ViewController.swift**, add the following code under the **Scene Management** section:

```swift
override func touchesBegan(_ touches: Set<UITouch>,
  with event: UIEvent?) {
  DispatchQueue.main.async {
    // 1
    if let touchLocation = touches.first?.location(
      in: self.sceneView) {
      if let hit = self.sceneView.hitTest(touchLocation,
        options: nil).first {
        // 2
        if hit.node.name == "Touch" {
          // 3
          let billboardNode = hit.node.childNode(
            withName: "Billboard", recursively: false)
          billboardNode?.isHidden = false
        }
        // 4
        if hit.node.name == "Billboard" {
          hit.node.isHidden = true
        }
      }
    }
  }
}
```

Here's what's happening:

1. This takes the first onscreen touch location, then performs a hit test to determine if any node has been touched in AR space. You're only interested in the first node.

2. You're only interested in nodes named **Touch**.

3. This locates the child node named **Billboard** and sets its state to visible.

4. If the node wasn't a **Touch** node but it was a **Billboard** node, it means the user touched a visible Billboard and wants to dismiss it. You then simply set the Billboard node back to a hidden state.

Enabling statistics & debugging (optional)

When dealing with problems, it's extremely helpful to enable the scene statistics and debugging information.

> **Note**: This step is an optional step you can use to debug ARKit and SceneKit scenes. Don't forget to turn it off again when you're done testing.

Add the following to the bottom of `initScene()`:

```
// 1
sceneView.showsStatistics = true
// 2
sceneView.debugOptions = [
  ARSCNDebugOptions.showFeaturePoints,
  ARSCNDebugOptions.showCreases,
  ARSCNDebugOptions.showWorldOrigin,
  ARSCNDebugOptions.showBoundingBoxes,
  ARSCNDebugOptions.showWireframe]
```

Here's what's happening:

1. To enable statistics, you simply set `showStatistics` to `true`.

2. To debug a particular scene, just provide the list of debugging options as an array.

Do a quick build and run to test it out. You should notice a bar at the bottom of the screen with a little + symbol. Press it to open the SceneKit statistics panel.

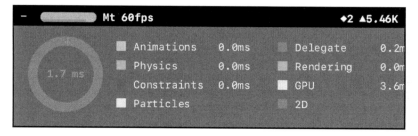

Here's what you see:

- At the top-left, a display of the current **rendering technology** shows **Mt**, short for Metal. Remember SceneKit was built on top of Metal, so that's perfect.
- Next to that, you see the **current frame rate**. A frame rate of **60fps** means that SceneKit is currently rendering the scene 60 times in a single second. If this number drops below 30fps, you should probably optimize the elements in your scene.
- The ◆ shows the total number of **draw calls per frame**.
- The ▲ shows the total **polygons per frame**.
- The big circle at the bottom-left shows the current **frame time** with a color legend of each component and their total time.

Adding the final touches

You're basically done, there are just a few tiny housecleaning issues that need to be done to ensure you handle every situation correctly.

Add the following lines to `startApp()`:

```
self.arPortNode.isHidden = true
self.focusNode.isHidden = true
```

This will ensure that both the focus node and the airport node start in a hidden state.

Add the following lines of code to `resetApp()`:

```
self.arPortNode.isHidden = true
```

This checks that the airport node returns to a hidden state when the AR experience restarts.

There's one final issue you need to resolve: The AR experience is simply way too big. You need to scale it down a bit so it will fit into the predicted footprint, as indicated by the focus node.

Open **art.scnassets/Scenes/ARPortScene.scn** and select **ARPort** in the **Scene graph**. Open the Node inspector and set the **Transforms Scale** to **(x: 0.75, y: 0.75, z: 0.75)**.

This scales the entire AR experience down to **75%** of its previous size. Now, it should fit on your dining room table!

Bam! Just like that, you're all done. Do one final build and run to reap the rewards of your hard work.

You'll notice that the AR experience is slightly smaller than before. Now, tapping the runway will show a pop-up with departure and arrival information. Tap the pop-up to dismiss it. Fantastic!

Key points

Congratulations, you've reached the end of this chapter and section, and you've created a super cool AR experience using SceneKit with ARKit.

Before signing off, take a look at some final key points:

- **SceneKit Asset Catalogs**: It's super easy to import 3D content into your SceneKit-based projects with an Asset Catalog. Best of all, the Asset Catalog is just a folder that can be shared, which keeps the code separate from the graphics.
- **Focus Node**: With basic ray casting, you can easily add a focus node to your AR experience, showing the user exactly what they're interacting with.
- **Billboards**: Adding billboard constraints to nodes is child's play. Now those nodes always face the camera.
- **SceneKit Scenes**: Scenes are simple to create and build. You can drag and drop primitive shapes from the Object Library, or you can reference other scenes with custom objects in them.
- **Lights & Shadows**: Adding lights to a scene brings that scene to life. Lights are especially important if you want the objects to cast shadows.
- **Shadow Catchers**: You can catch an object's shadow with a basic Plane node that uses a special Shadows Only shader as a material.
- **Presenting Scenes**: SceneKit makes it easy to load a scene from the Asset Catalog. Displaying that scene is a simple as adding it to the main scene as a child node.
- **Interaction**: With the power of hit testing, you can quickly add scene interaction to any AR experience.
- **Statistics & Debugging**: When things don't make sense, adding statistics and debugging information makes all the difference in finding weird bugs.

Go show your friends your awesome AR airport, but don't forget to come back for the next and final project. This time around you'll get to learn all about how to create collaborative AR experiences. See you there!

Section VII: ECS & Collaborative Experiences (Bonus Section)

In this section, you'll create a multiplayer AR shared experience using RealityKit. In this experience, two players can play a basic Knots & Crosses game on separate devices.

Chapter 17: ECS & Collaborative Experiences

In the early days of ARKit, it quickly became apparent that something important was missing: the ability to share augmented reality experiences among multiple users.

Later versions of ARKit addressed the issue by introducing `ARWorldMap`. The map contains a space-mapping state along with a set of anchors from a world-tracking AR session. This map can be shared, allowing multiple users to experience persistent AR anchors within the same space.

With the assistance of a peer-to-peer network, multiple users can share an `ARWorldMap` in real time, creating a collaborative experience. Using ARKit, the process is somewhat painful, requiring vast amounts of manual labor from a coding perspective.

Apple created a fantastic ARKit example project that you can explore. Find the project here: https://apple.co/31ltm2u

However, since iOS 13, you've been able to pair RealityKit with ARKit to automate most of the manual effort that ARKit-based apps typically require.

In this chapter, you'll create a modern take on the classic Tic-Tac-Toe game and deliver a RealityKit-based collaborative experience. The new project will borrow from Apple's ARKit example project, but will mainly focus on the RealityKit side of things.

It's time to get going!

Exploring the project

There's a starter project waiting for you in the **starter/XOXO** folder. The project is a basic Swift-based app that uses a classic style storyboard UI.

Load the project in Xcode so you can take a quick tour of the important components within.

ViewController.swift

Open **ViewController.swift**. By now, you're very familiar with the inner workings of the `ViewController`.

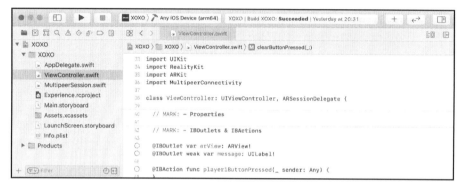

This is where you'll place most of your code. You'll also find pre-allocated stubs within the code which not only keep things organized, but also make placing code easier.

MultipeerController.swift

Open **MultipeerController.swift**.

This is an exact copy of the file from Apple's ARKit-based example project. It's a nice little class that handles all the network management for you. Why reinvent the wheel, right?

Main.storyboard

Open **Main.storyboard** and flip the orientation to landscape.

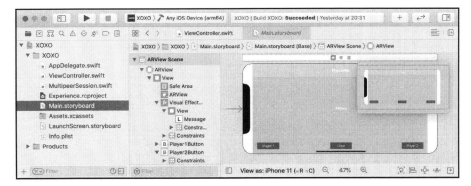

It contains an ARView with an area at the top that you'll use to send messages to the user. You'll also see three buttons at the bottom of the view. These will let the user choose to be **Player1** or **Player2** or to clear the game board with the **Clear** button.

Also, note that these components are already connected to their @IBActions and @IBOutlets, which are located within the ViewController.

Info.plist

Open **Info.plist**.

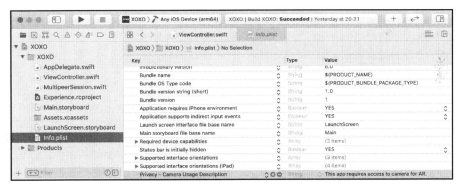

This is where you'll ask for network permissions. Note that **Camera Usage Description** is already set, so your app will ask for permission to use the camera when it starts.

Creating the AR View

Now that you've gotten the basics out of the way, you'll start filling in the missing pieces, beginning with the AR View.

Setting the player's color

Add the following variable to the **Properties** section:

```
var playerColor = UIColor.blue
```

This property will indicate the player's color. **Player1** will be **blue** and **Player2** will be **red**.

Next, add the following to player1ButtonPressed(_:):

```
playerColor = UIColor.blue
```

This sets the player's color to **blue** when the player chooses **Player1**.

Similarly, add this to player2ButtonPressed(_:):

```
playerColor = UIColor.red
```

This sets the player's color to **red** when they choose **Player2**.

Sending messages

Add the following helper function to **Helper Functions**:

```
func sendMessage(_ message: String) {
  DispatchQueue.main.async {
    self.message.text = message
  }
}
```

With this function in place, you'll be able to send messages to keep the user informed of all crucial events and states.

Creating the AR configuration

You start all AR experiences by creating an `ARConfiguration` and running the AR session. Well, this AR experience is no different.

Add the following call to `viewDidAppear()` under **AR View Functions**:

```
initARView()
```

This generates an error because the function doesn't exist yet. Fear not, you'll fix that next.

Add the following function to **AR View Functions**:

```
func initARView() {
  arView.session.delegate = self
  arView.automaticallyConfigureSession = false
  let arConfiguration = ARWorldTrackingConfiguration()
  arConfiguration.planeDetection = [.horizontal]
  arConfiguration.environmentTexturing = .automatic
  arView.session.run(arConfiguration)
}
```

This ensures that `ViewController` is the session delegate. It then creates and runs an AR session with a standard `ARWorldTrackingConfiguration` that detects **horizontal** planes.

For good measure, do a build and run test, just to make sure everything's in working order.

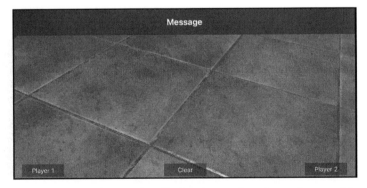

The AR session is active and scanning for horizontal surfaces, but nothing much else is happening. There are a few buttons to press, but no feedback yet. For your next step, you'll actually put something in the scene.

What is ECS?

When using the RealityKit framework to create content for your AR experiences, it's important to note that the framework runs a CPU-based entity-component system (ECS) to manage physics, animations, audio processing and network synchronization. The framework then relies on Metal for GPU-based multithreaded rendering.

For your first step, take a look at a typical RealityKit-based experience.

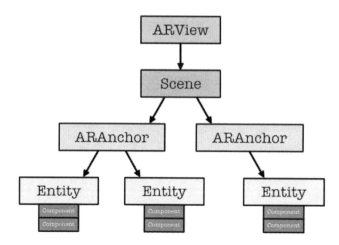

There are four main elements you need when dealing with an AR experience based on RealityKit:

- **ARView**: This is your window into the world of AR, serving as RealityKit's entry point. It's essentially just a view that goes into your app's view hierarchy.

- **Scene**: The scene, which is owned by `ARView`, holds all the virtual content of your AR experience.

- **ARAnchor**: Anchors describe how your AR content relates to the real world. You assign a target to an anchor, and when the app finds an appropriate target, it creates the anchor and attaches it to the real world.

- **Entity**: Entities represent the virtual content of an AR experience — its building blocks. Entities consist of **Components**, which define their behavior. It's also important to point out that entities can contain other entities, forming a parent-child-like hierarchy.

Predefined entities

With RealityKit, you can easily create your own custom entities with custom behaviors based on the various components you add to them.

You can also choose from a list of predefined entities:

- **AnchorEntity**: An entity with an anchor component. It attaches itself to the real world and automatically tracks its target based on the anchoring type you've defined.
- **ModelEntity**: Contains geometry, materials, animation and physics components. It's commonly used to represent the visual parts of your AR experience.
- **PointLight, SpotLight & DirectionalLight**: Produce various lighting conditions for virtual content.
- **PerspectiveCamera**: Provides a virtual camera that establishes the rendering perspective.
- **TriggerVolume**: Defines a 3D shape that detects when other objects enter or exit the defined space.
- **BodyTrackedEntity**: Animates a virtual character within an AR scene based on real-time tracking data from a real person.

Creating the game board

Now that you have some background, it's time to create some of your very own entities, starting with the game board.

You'll construct the game board from scratch using primitive shapes. It will contain:

- A vertical grid bar
- A horizontal grid bar
- Nine tiles

The tiles allow the players to interact with the game board. When the player touches a tile, that tile changes into the player's chosen color.

Add the following variables to the **Properties** section:

```
var gridModelEntityX:ModelEntity?
var gridModelEntityY:ModelEntity?
var tileModelEntity:ModelEntity?
```

These are the core entities that will construct the entire game board.

Creating the model entities

Look carefully at the game board and you can see that the entire board is constructed out of just three distinct shapes: the two grid bars and the square tiles. You'll create those shapes next.

Add a call to the following function at the bottom of `viewDidAppear(_:)`:

```
initModelEntities()
```

This generates an error, which you'll fix by adding the following function to **Model Entity Functions**:

```
func initModelEntities() {
  // 1
  gridModelEntityX = ModelEntity(
    mesh: .generateBox(size: SIMD3(x: 0.3, y: 0.01, z: 0.01)),
    materials: [SimpleMaterial(color: .white, isMetallic: false)]
  )
  // 2
  gridModelEntityY = ModelEntity(
    mesh: .generateBox(size: SIMD3(x: 0.01, y: 0.01, z: 0.3)),
    materials: [SimpleMaterial(color: .white, isMetallic: false)]
  )
  // 3
  tileModelEntity = ModelEntity(
    mesh: .generateBox(size: SIMD3(x: 0.07, y: 0.01, z: 0.07)),
```

```
    materials: [SimpleMaterial(color: .gray, isMetallic: true)]
  )
  // 4
  tileModelEntity!.generateCollisionShapes(recursive: false)
}
```

Now, take a closer look at the three model entities you're constructing here:

1. The Tic-Tac-Toe grid consists of two types of grid bars. Here, you define the vertical grid bar with a mesh component generated from a box that measures (`X:30cm, Y:1cm, Z:1cm`). It assigns a single white plastic material to the bar.

2. This defines the horizontal grid bar with a mesh component generated from a box that measures (`X:1cm, Y:1cm, Z:30cm`). It also assigns a single white plastic material to the bar.

3. This defines the tile with a mesh component generated from a box that measures (`X:7cm, Y:1cm, Z:7cm`). It assigns a single gray metallic material to the tile.

4. To interact with elements in the scene, those elements require a collision component. Here, you generate a collision shaped component for the tile model entity by using the mesh component. Now, you'll be able to hit test against the tiles.

Cloning model entities

Now that you've created the three main shapes, you'll use them to construct the game board. Instead of re-creating each element from scratch, you'll clone the original entities.

Add the following helper function to **Model Entity Functions**:

```
func cloneModelEntity(_ modelEntity: ModelEntity,
  position: SIMD3<Float>) -> ModelEntity {
  let newModelEntity = modelEntity.clone(recursive: false)
  newModelEntity.position = position
  return newModelEntity
}
```

This nifty helper function lets you clone an existing `ModelEntity` with the option to give it a new **position**.

Adding the grid

Now, you're going to use the helper function above to create the grid. Add the following function to **Model Entity Functions**:

```
func addGameBoardAnchor(transform: simd_float4x4) {
  // 1
  let arAnchor = ARAnchor(name: "XOXO Grid", transform:
transform)
  let anchorEntity = AnchorEntity(anchor: arAnchor)
  // 2
  anchorEntity.addChild(cloneModelEntity(gridModelEntityY!,
    position: SIMD3(x: 0.05, y: 0, z: 0)))
  anchorEntity.addChild(cloneModelEntity(gridModelEntityY!,
    position: SIMD3(x: -0.05, y: 0, z: 0)))
  anchorEntity.addChild(cloneModelEntity(gridModelEntityX!,
    position: SIMD3(x: 0.0, y: 0, z: 0.05)))
  anchorEntity.addChild(cloneModelEntity(gridModelEntityX!,
    position: SIMD3(x: 0.0, y: 0, z: -0.05)))
}
```

Now, take a closer look:

1. The entire game board is connected to an `AnchorEntity` that forms the root entity of the game board. Here, you create an `AnchorEntity` with an `ARAnchor` using the provided transform value for the anchor's position.

2. Here, the nifty new cloning function creates two vertical bars and two horizontal bars to form the grid for the Tic-Tac-Toe experience. All the entities become children of the root `anchorEntity`.

Adding the tiles

With the grid out of the way, you need to add the tiles to the game board. There are nine slots to fill.

Add the following to the bottom of `addGameBoardAnchor(_:)`:

```
anchorEntity.addChild(cloneModelEntity(tileModelEntity!,
  position: SIMD3(x: -0.1, y: 0, z: -0.1)))
anchorEntity.addChild(cloneModelEntity(tileModelEntity!,
  position: SIMD3(x: 0, y: 0, z: -0.1)))
anchorEntity.addChild(cloneModelEntity(tileModelEntity!,
  position: SIMD3(x: 0.1, y: 0, z: -0.1)))
anchorEntity.addChild(cloneModelEntity(tileModelEntity!,
  position: SIMD3(x: -0.1, y: 0, z: 0)))
anchorEntity.addChild(cloneModelEntity(tileModelEntity!,
  position: SIMD3(x: 0, y: 0, z: 0)))
```

```
anchorEntity.addChild(cloneModelEntity(tileModelEntity!,
    position: SIMD3(x: 0.1, y: 0, z: 0)))
anchorEntity.addChild(cloneModelEntity(tileModelEntity!,
    position: SIMD3(x: -0.1, y: 0, z: 0.1)))
anchorEntity.addChild(cloneModelEntity(tileModelEntity!,
    position: SIMD3(x: 0, y: 0, z: 0.1)))
anchorEntity.addChild(cloneModelEntity(tileModelEntity!,
    position: SIMD3(x: 0.1, y: 0, z: 0.1)))
```

This follows the same process as before, making cloned copies of the original tile. It places each clone at a different position to fill the 9×9 grid. Also, note that each tile becomes a child of the root `anchorEntity`.

Adding the anchor

Now that you've now completed the grid and all the tiles, your next step is to add the game board to the AR scene.

Add the following to the bottom of `addGameBoardAnchor(_:)`:

```
// 1
anchorEntity.anchoring = AnchoringComponent(arAnchor)
// 2
arView.scene.addAnchor(anchorEntity)
// 3
arView.session.add(anchor: arAnchor)
```

This creates a new game board and places it in the scene. It also anchors the game board to the surface at the provided position.

Placing content

Now that your game board is ready to place in the scene, you need some user input to know where to place it. All the user needs to do is tap the horizontal surface and the game board should appear in that position. Your next step is to ensure the app recognizes the user's tap.

Creating a tap gesture

You'll start by creating a basic tap gesture to handle user touch input.

Add the following call to the bottom of `viewDidAppear(_:)`:

```
initGestures()
```

This generates an error, but you can easily fix it by adding the following function to **Gesture Functions**:

```
func initGestures() {
  // 1
  let tap = UITapGestureRecognizer(
    target: self,
    action: #selector(handleTap))
  // 2
  self.arView.addGestureRecognizer(tap)
}
```

Now, take a closer look:

1. This creates a new tap gesture recognizer, nominating the `ViewController` as the **target** and saying that `handleTap()` should be called when the user taps the screen.

2. This adds the newly created gesture to the AR view.

Handling tap gestures

But hang, on there's an error. You still need to define `handleTap()`.

Add the following functions to **Gesture Functions**:

```
@objc func handleTap(recognizer: UITapGestureRecognizer?) {
}
```

Excellent, now you just need to add the code to handle the actual tap.

Getting the touch location

After the user taps the screen, you'll cast a ray into the scene to see where on the surface the tap actually occurred. This lets you position the game board just where they want it.

Add the following to the top of handleTap(recognizer:):

```
guard let touchLocation =
  recognizer?.location(in: self.arView) else { return }
```

This gets the onscreen touch location from the gesture recognizer.

Tapping a surface

Now, to perform the actual ray-cast into the AR scene.

Add the following code to bottom of handleTap(recognizer:):

```
let results = self.arView.raycast(
  from: touchLocation,
  allowing: .estimatedPlane,
  alignment: .horizontal)

if let firstResult = results.first {
  self.addGameBoardAnchor(transform: firstResult.worldTransform)
} else {
  self.message.text = "[WARNING] No surface detected!"
}
```

This casts a ray into the scene, looking for the closest horizontal surface. When the ray finds a target, it adds the game board to the scene at the exact location where the ray hits the surface.

Tapping a tile

OK, now that the game board is visible in the scene, what's next? Well, when the user touches a tile, that tile should change to the player's color.

To check if the user tapped a tile, you'll piggyback on the tap gesture handler.

Add the following code to the top of `handleTap(recognizer:)`, just after the `guard` statement:

```
if let hitEntity = self.arView.entity(at: touchLocation) {
  let modelEntity = hitEntity as! ModelEntity
    modelEntity.model?.materials = [
      SimpleMaterial(color: self.playerColor,
        isMetallic: true)]
  return
}
```

Instead of using another ray cast, this uses `arView.entity(at:)` to locate a touched entity in the scene. If it finds a hit, it simply updates the material color to the user's color.

For `arView.entity(at:)` to successfully detect contact with entities in the AR scene, the entities must have a collision shape component. If you recall, you did that when you created the tile entity in `initModelEntities()`.

Okay, enough coding for now, do a build and run to test out the current state of affairs.

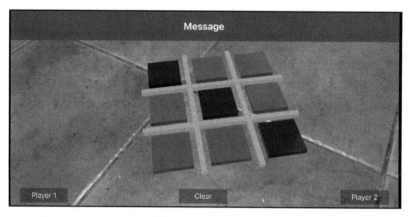

When you tap the surface, the cool board game gets placed right where you tapped. When you choose Player 1 and then tap a tile, that tile turns blue. When you tap a tile after choosing Player 2, that tile turns red. You've essentially built a pass-and-play version of the old classic Tic-Tac-Toe game with a modern twist. Fantastic!

But playing with just one device is no fun. Next, you'll let each player play on their own device.

Collaborative experiences

When multiple people share an augmented reality experience from their own personal viewpoints on separate devices, it's known as a **collaborative experience**. To achieve such an experience, all the devices should be connected to one another via a local network or Bluetooth. The devices share an AR world map, which localizes each device within the same space. During an active collaborative session, entities in the augmented space synchronize across all the other devices.

Thanks to the power of RealityKit, achieving a collaborative experience is actually easy. The first thing you need to do is to create a multi-peer network between the devices.

Creating a multi-peer network with MCSession

Thankfully, all the hard work is already done, thanks to `MultipeerSession`, which is part of your project. It acts as a basic wrapper class for `MCSession`, which is the network session class that connects multiple peers.

The network session can **browse** for available **hosts**, and it can also **advertise** itself as an available **host**. The browser will search for advertisers. When it finds one, the browser then sends an invitation to join the network advertiser's network session.

The advertiser then handles the invitation and connects the devices to the same network session. Once it establishes a connection, the network session will manage communication between the connected devices.

> **Note:** `MultipeerSession` offers various event handlers that you can tap into to control the flow of network session events.

Adding multi-peer connectivity

Now that the network is ready, you'll create the multi-peer session.

Open **ViewController.swift** and add the following variables under **Properties**:

```
var multipeerSession: MultipeerSession?
var peerSessionIDs = [MCPeerID: String]()
var sessionIDObservation: NSKeyValueObservation?
```

So what are these variables used for?

- **multipeerSession**: Holds the instance of `MultipeerSession` that you'll create.
- **peerSessionIDs**: A list of peer IDs (Strings) that will keep track of the connected peers. You'll maintain this list of IDs manually.
- **sessionIDObservation**: Uses the observation pattern to monitor your own session ID, in case it changes over time.

Add the following function call to the bottom of viewDidAppear(_:):

```
initMultipeerSession()
```

This will generate an error, which you'll resolve by adding the following code under **Multipeer Session Functions**:

```
func initMultipeerSession()
{
    multipeerSession = MultipeerSession(
        receivedDataHandler: receivedData,
        peerJoinedHandler: peerJoined,
        peerLeftHandler: peerLeft,
        peerDiscoveredHandler: peerDiscovered)
}

func receivedData(_ data: Data, from peer: MCPeerID) {
}

func peerDiscovered(_ peer: MCPeerID) -> Bool {
}

func peerJoined(_ peer: MCPeerID) {
}

func peerLeft(_ peer: MCPeerID) {
}
```

This creates an instance of `MultipeerSession` and provides it with event handlers for all possible network session events.

Internally, `MultipeerSession` will start both a **browser** and an **advertiser**. It will operate in both modes, as a host and as a client connecting to other hosts. RealityKit requires this to perform the synchronization.

Handling session ID changes

When a peer connects or when your session ID changes, you need to inform the connected peers of your current peer ID.

Add the following helper function to **Multipeer Session Functions**:

```
private func sendARSessionIDTo(peers: [MCPeerID]) {
  guard let multipeerSession = multipeerSession else { return }
  let idString = arView.session.identifier.uuidString
  let command = "SessionID:" + idString
  if let commandData = command.data(using: .utf8) {
    multipeerSession.sendToPeers(commandData,
        reliably: true,
        peers: peers)
  }
}
```

This nifty helper function lets you send your own session ID to the other connected peers, making sure you keep them up-to-date.

Now, add the following to the top of initMultipeerSession():

```
sessionIDObservation = observe(\.arView.session.identifier,
  options: [.new]) { object, change in
    print("Current SessionID: \(change.newValue!)")
    guard let multipeerSession = self.multipeerSession else
    { return }
    self.sendARSessionIDTo(peers:
multipeerSession.connectedPeers)
}
```

This uses the observer pattern to monitor your current session ID. Should it change, this will ensure the other connected peers are informed of your latest session ID.

You'll handle the network session events next.

Handling the "peer" discovered event

When the network session discovers a new peer, it triggers peerDiscovered(_:), asking it for permission to allow the new peer to connect.

Add the following to peerDiscovered(_:):

```
guard let multipeerSession = multipeerSession else
{ return false }
```

```
sendMessage("Peer discovered!")

if multipeerSession.connectedPeers.count > 2 {
  sendMessage("[WARNING] Max connections reached!")
  return false
} else {
  return true
}
```

Here, you build in a restriction on the number of active connected peers allowed at once time. The code above simply checks that the total number of connected peers is under the allowed amount. If so, the peer is allowed to connect; otherwise, it's rejected and the user gets a message that there are too many connections.

Handling the "peer joined" event

When the peer is allowed to connect, the network session will trigger peerJoined(_:).

Add the following to peerJoined(_:):

```
sendMessage("Hold phones together...")
sendARSessionIDTo(peers: [peer])
```

As soon as a peer joins, it's good time to inform the users to hold their phones close together. It's also the perfect time to send your own session id to the peer who just joined so that they can also keep track of you in their list of peers.

Handling the "peer left" event

When a peer leaves, you need to update peerSessionIDs. To do this, add the following to peerLeft(_:):

```
sendMessage("Peer left!")
peerSessionIDs.removeValue(forKey: peer)
```

This removes the peer from peerSessionIDs, maintaining the list at all times.

Configuring RealityKit for collaboration

Well, that's all you need to do to create a multi-peer network, but you're not quite done yet. You still need to configure RealityKit for collaboration.

Enabling collaboration

To use collaboration, you need to enable it when you create the AR configuration. Do this by adding the following line of code to `initARView()`, just before running the AR session:

```
arConfiguration.isCollaborationEnabled = true
```

Enabling collaboration will start sharing collaboration data with connected peers. Collaboration data contains information about detected surfaces, device positions and added anchors.

Setting the synchronization service

When you use RealityKit, you have to synchronize all of its entities and their components with all the connected peers.

Open **MultipeerSession.swift** and add the following extension to the bottom of the file:

```
extension MultipeerSession {
  public var multipeerConnectivityService:
    MultipeerConnectivityService? {
      return try? MultipeerConnectivityService(
        session: self.session)
  }
}
```

Look at `MultipeerSession` and you'll notice that that actual session instance, `MCSession`, is kept private. This extension allows you to create a multi-peer connectivity session, while still keeping the session private.

Next, back in **ViewController.swift**, add the following to the bottom of `initMultipeerSession()`:

```
// 1
guard let multipeerConnectivityService =
  multipeerSession!.multipeerConnectivityService else {
    fatalError("[FATAL ERROR] Unable to create Sync Service!")
```

```
    }
// 2
arView.scene.synchronizationService =
multipeerConnectivityService
self.message.text = "Waiting for peers..."
```

Take a closer look:

1. With the extension function in place, this makes sure that you get a valid multipeer session service from `MultipeerSession`.

2. This registers the synchronization service. Now, RealityKit will keep all the `Codable` objects in sync. This includes entities along with all their components.

Handling a successful connection

Now that everything's in place, once a new peer successfully joins, RealityKit will create an `ARParticipationAnchor` for that peer.

Add the following function to **Multipeer Session Functions**:

```
func session(_ session: ARSession, didAdd anchors: [ARAnchor]) {
  for anchor in anchors {
    if let participantAnchor = anchor as? ARParticipantAnchor {
      self.message.text = "Peer connected!"
      let anchorEntity = AnchorEntity(anchor: participantAnchor)
      arView.scene.addAnchor(anchorEntity)
    }
  }
}
```

Here, you use `session(_:didAdd)` — which is part of the `ARSessionDelegate` protocol — to check if a newly-added anchor is an `ARParticipationAnchor`. If it is, a peer has just successfully connected and an active collaborative experience is in progress. Excellent!

Requesting network permissions

Oh, you're not quite done yet. There's one last thing that you have to do and that's to request network permissions.

Open **Info.plist** and add the following to it:

- **Privacy — Local Network Usage Description**: Set its value to something descriptive like: **This app requires access to the network for Collaboration.**
- **Bonjour services**: Add two sub-items to it. Set **item 0** to **_ar-collab._tcp** and set **item 1** to **_ar-collab._udp**.

The result should look like this:

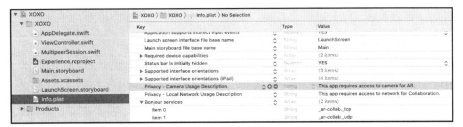

The value `ar-collab` is a hard-coded string value defined within `MultipeerSession` that's used when creating the **browser** and **advertiser services**.

Bonjour services gives permission to use that specific service type name.

> **Note**: Your app will crash if you've failed to request network permission. Continue with caution!

Time to build, run and test out your collaborative experience.

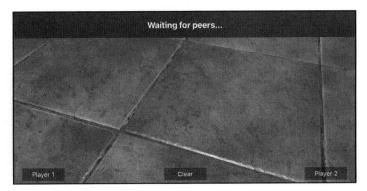

The app starts and now asks for network permission. Nothing else has changed, except for the message at the top stating that it's **Waiting for peers…**. Oh, of course — this is supposed to be a collaborative experience! :]

Before grabbing a friend, there's one *final* thing you have to set up for the entire experience to function as intended.

Managing ownership

During a collaborative experience, when you create an entity, you become the owner of that entity. Should another peer attempt to modify an entity that belongs to you, they'll be blocked.

This is a great locking mechanism to control who's allowed to modify entities within the AR scene. Without these controls, you'd have utter chaos.

However, this means you need to add ownership management to your app.

Enabling automatic ownership

To keep things simple, when another peer requests ownership of an entity that belongs to you, you'll simply transfer ownership to that peer automatically.

Add the following line of code to the bottom of `addGameBoardAnchor(_:)`, just before adding the `anchorEntity` to the scene:

```
anchorEntity.synchronization?.ownershipTransferMode
  = .autoAccept
```

This simply sets `ownershipTransferMode` to automatically accept ownership requests. Now, when a peer interacts with a tile, they first need to request ownership of that tile before trying to change its color.

Requesting ownership

Now, you need to make sure you request ownership when you tap on a tile.

In `handleTap(recognizer:)`, replace the previous entire `hitEntity` code block with this new one:

```
if let hitEntity = self.arView.entity(at: touchLocation) {
  if hitEntity.isOwner {
```

```
      let modelEntity = hitEntity as! ModelEntity
      modelEntity.model?.materials = [
        SimpleMaterial(color: self.playerColor,
          isMetallic: true)]
    } else {
      hitEntity.requestOwnership { result in
        if result == .granted {
          let modelEntity = hitEntity as! ModelEntity
          modelEntity.model?.materials = [
            SimpleMaterial(color: self.playerColor,
              isMetallic: true)]
        }
      }
    }
    return
}
```

Previously, you simply modified the tile color. This time around, you first check to see if you're the owner of the tile. If you are, no worries, you can change the tile color. If not, you first have to request ownership. Once granted, ownership of the tile now belongs to you and you can change the tile color.

Removing anchors

As a final touch, when you've played a few games with a friend, it would be nice to clear out the playing field so that you can play some more.

Add the following helper function to **Helper Functions**:

```
func removeAnchors() {
  guard let frame = arView.session.currentFrame else { return }
  for anchor in frame.anchors {
    arView.session.remove(anchor: anchor)
  }
  sendMessage("All anchors removed!")
}
```

Then add a call to it in `clearButtonPressed_:)`:

```
removeAnchors()
```

And now do one final build and run. This time around, make sure that the app's installed on more than one device.

The sequence of events should flow as follows:

1. **Device A** starts and states that it's **Waiting for peers…**.

2. **Device B** starts and also states that it's **Waiting for peers…**.

3. When the two devices come into close proximity to one another, both will indicate that they've **Discovered a peer**. At this point, hold the two devices close together to establish a collaborative session.

4. If all goes well, the collaborative session begins and both devices indicate that a **Peer connected!**

5. **Device A** chooses to be **Player 1** and **Device B** chooses to be **Player 2**.

6. Either device can now add a game board to the scene by tapping a flat surface. The players can now take turns and play the ultimate game of Tic-Tac-Toe.

7. When the game board gets messy, simply **Clear** the space and place a new game board into the scene.

Key points

Congratulations, you've reached the end of this chapter and section. You can find a copy of the project in its final state under **final/XOXO**.

Do a quick rewind and see what you learned:

- **ECS**: You learned about entity-component systems and how to create your very own entities, each with their own set of components that define the behavior of the entity.
- **Predefined Entities**: You learned that RealityKit comes with a whole collection of predefined entities that are commonly used within RealityKit-based AR experiences.
- **Custom Entities**: You also created your own custom entities and controlled which components you added to them.
- **Cloning Entities**: Cloning an entity is super simple and lightens a repetitive workload.
- **Collaborative Experiences**: Creating a collaborative experience for RealityKit is straightforward. All you need is an active peer-to-peer network session. Then you just configure a few basic settings and you're up and running.
- **Synchronization**: RealityKit will automatically synchronize all `Codable` objects for you over the network. This includes all entities with their components.
- **Ownership**: When dealing with entities in a collaborative session, you have to request ownership of that entity before you can modify it. Luckily, there are a few settings to enable that make this a breeze.

Well done, grasshopper, you've earned a well-deserved break. Share your app with all your friends and enjoy some competitive Tic-Tac-Toe. See you on the flip side! :]

Conclusion

What a fantastic journey it's been! From exploring what AR is and why it matters to diving deep into the technology and frameworks that you can use to bring your AR experiences to life.

By putting the book concepts to practice, creating beautiful, immersive AR worlds for your users to explore will become second nature. Not only that, but you'll also be able to respond quickly to changing requirements as the technology expands and matures.

We hope the ideas you saw in this book inspire you to explore and enjoy AR like never before!

If you have any questions or comments as you work through this book, please stop by our forums at https://forums.raywenderlich.com and look for the particular forum category for this book.

Thank you again for purchasing this book. Your continued support is what makes the books, tutorials, videos and other things we do at raywenderlich.com possible. We truly appreciate it!

– Chris Language, Sandra Grauschopf, and Tammy Coron

The *Apple Augmented Reality by Tutorials* team

Printed in Great Britain
by Amazon